Tamm's Textbook Tools

AP* Human Geography student worksheets and course materials

James M. Rubenstein's
The Cultural Landscape⁺
11th edition (orange cover)

COURSEPAK SERIES A　　　　　　　　　**INDEPENDENTLY MADE**

David Tamm

*Advanced Placement program and AP are registered trademarks of the College Board, which was not involved in the production of, and does not endorse, this product.

⁺The Cultural Landscape 11th edition is written by James M. Rubenstein and published by Pearson. These parties were not involved in the production of, and do not endorse, this product.

Cover Image: *The Fountain of Indolence* (1834), by J.M.W. Turner

Contents

This resource book is organized in the following way to integrate with Rubenstein's *The Cultural Landscape* 11th edition (orange cover)

Part 1: Vocab Lists

Part 2: People Lists

Part 3: Chapter Assignments

Part 4: Additional Vocab from Other Texts and Online

Addenda: Crash Course Response Forms, Test Correction Sheet, Film Review Form, Documentary Review Form, History of Geography in Schools, Final Word

Copyright © 2015

Teachers are fully licensed by the copyright holder to copy individual worksheets out of this book in whatever quantity is needed for classroom use. Students may also order a full workbook as a consumable to write in throughout the year. These materials may not be distributed online in any form or shared with other teachers without expressed written permission.

When given as a full workbook, this material improves content coherency, student enjoyment, parent appreciation, and teacher satisfaction."

-State of Florida Certified Teacher

"Perfect if there's a sub"

"A giant leap for studentkind"

"Awesome, usable resources!"

"Spend 1 hour's pay, save hundreds of hours of planning time!"

Suggested Use

Manic Moon Day
It is recommended that students have a lecture overview of the key points in each chapter, take notes, and discuss the concepts involved. Even though teachers are discouraged in some parts of the country from lecturing, the speed of the AP Human Geography course necessitates some direct teacher-student transmission of content. The part 1 vocab forms could be used as a guide during the discussion or even as a guide for notes.

Textbook Tiw's Day
Most school districts encourage pair or group work. This can be used to positive effect if students diligently mine the textbook (or a review book) in class and either jigsaw the chapter, presenting their take on part of the whole, or jointly venture to find answers to the specific problems in geography. Such classroom activities for each chapter are located in Part 2 of this coursepak.

Writing Woden's Day
As we know, the AP* Human Geography curriculum is reading and writing intensive. A good way to build up key thinking processes and techniques helpful in expressing oneself in writing is to brainstorm and diagram solutions to FRQs appropriate to each chapter. Another helpful way to do writings is good old-fashioned reading comprehension and short answers, but as many teachers know, the content of the passages is key to student growth and success. If it isn't interesting, you might as well be pulling teeth. Luckily, Human Geography has a great potential interest value. If you find the current work helpful and of high enough quality for the Monday and Tuesday assignments, you may want to obtain a companion volume to this book, *Tamm's Textbook Tools Coursepak Series B: Readings, Writings and Online Activities*, or *Coursepak C: The Grand Tour of Human Geography,* on *Amazon.com* or another platform.

Technetronic Thor's Day
Teachers are tasked with bringing technology into the classroom, whether in the form of a laptop cart, taking students to a media lab, or having them use mobile devices or *iPads*. *Kahoot.it* is popular as a Jeopardy-style review game, joining *Quizlet* and a vast number of other review materials available online. A good directory to websites usable with AP Human Geography classes, including the Rubenstein textbook site with its own activities, is located at Antarcticaedu.com/Geo.htm. Included in the addendum to this volume is a Crash Course viewer response sheet that can be given as homework on Thursday nights, or completed as an in-class review assignment. *Coursepak B* has more online activities too.

Fantastic Freyja's Day
It is suggested that students take a 25-50-question test once a week. That means many of the chapters will have to be cut in half and tests made for each half. Cutting the chapters in half will get you 26 weeks of content, which is just about right. A 35 min. period should be reserved in class- or in some cases out- to do these weekly tests. If this happens on Friday, it is recommended students take home the Part I: Vocab and Part II: People for homework, due the following week. Doing the vocab is a good way to introduce the new chapter.

Suggested Year Plan

Rubenstein's 11th ed. (2013)
Nowadays

Week 1: Chapter 1a Basics
Week 2: Chapter 1b Basics
Week 3: Chapter 2a Population
Week 4: Chapter 2b Population
Week 5: Chapter 3a Migration
Week 6: Chapter 3b Migration
Week 7: Chapter 4a Culture
Week 8: Chapter 4b Culture
Week 9: Chapter 5a Language
Week 10: Chapter 5b Language
Week 11: Chapter 6a Religion
Week 12: Chapter 6b Religion
Week 13: Chapter 7a Ethnicity
Week 14: Chapter 7b Ethnicity
Week 15: Chapter 8a Political
Week 16: Chapter 8b Political
Week 17: Chapter 9a Development
Week 18: Chapter 9b Development
Week 19: Chapter 10a Agriculture
Week 20: Chapter 10b Agriculture
Week 21: Chapter 11a Industry
Week 22: Chapter 11b Industry
Week 23: Chapter 12a Services
Week 24: Chapter 12b Services
Week 25: Chapter 13a Urban
Week 26: Chapter 13b Urban

Huntington's *Human Geography* (1920)
Flashback

Human Geography
Effect of the Earth's Form and Motions
Continents and Man
Human Activities in Mountains and Plains
Influence of the Oceans
Use of Inland Waters
Soil and the Farmer
Metals and Civilization
Sources of Power
Climate and the Climatic Zones
Climate of Continent and Oceans
Climate and Human Energy
Earth's Garment of Vegetation
Vegetation and Man in the Warmest Regions
Life in Subtropical and Monsoon Regions
Modes of Life in Desert and Polar Regions
Irrigation
Man's Work in Regions of Cyclonic Storms
The World's Diet
Man's Changing Surroundings
Political Geography
International Relations

Part I

"Manic Monday"

Vocabulary

and "Textbook Tuesday"

Chapter Assignments

Pg. 5   1 - BASIC CONCEPTS – Keys 1/2   Name _____

Right now someone is making a map. And you're on it.

Geography _____

Two simple questions human geographers ask are:

1   2

Pic 5 (top): At right, draw the pattern of islands in the Polynesian Stick Chart:

What was the purpose for making this kind of chart?

_____

_____

_____

While we might not know the first geographer's name, we do know what they probably did. What was it?

_____

Map _____

Cartography _____

Pic 5 (bot.): On the nighttime map of Earth, what are two reasons some areas are unlit?

_____   _____

Eratosthenes _____

Ptolemy _____

Pei Xiu _____

Muhammad al-Idrisi _____

Martin Waldseemuller _____

Amerigo Vespucci _____

Abraham Ortelius _____

Atlas _____

Bernhardus Varenius _____

Map 6: What are three world regions shown on Eratosthenes' map?

I drew the first modern atlas: *Eratosthenes* *Al-Idrisi* *Ortelius*

Nearly 3,000 people died during Pearl Harbor, likewise on 9/11. Did more or fewer people die in the Hurricane Katrina disaster? _____

Pg. 7: What is the main tourist attraction in New Orleans? _____

Math: How many African-Americans left New Orleans after the disaster? _____

Map scale _____

Projection _____

Shape distortion _____

Distance distortion _____

Relative size distortion _____

Direction distortion _____

Equal area projection _____

Robinson projection _____

Mercator projection _____

Goode Homolosine projection _____

Pic 8: Give an example of the following:

　　　　map scale　　　　　　　　　　*written ratio*

Pic 9: Draw the *shape* of the world maps for each of the projections (don't worry about filling them in):

　　　　Mercator　　　　　　　　**Goode**　　　　　　　　**Robinson**

Advantages:

Disadvantages:

Meridian / longitude _____

Parallel / latitude _____

Degrees _____

GMT _____

Time zone _____

International Date Line _____

Map 10: The Prime Meridian and Equator intersect off the west coast of _____.

The Prime Meridian runs through _____ in England, where geographers drew the lines.

What prize did John Harrison win and why? _____

_____

What is the master reference time for all points on Earth? _____

On the exact opposite side of the world from the Prime Meridian is the _____

Map 11: List four of the first countries or islands to receive the cascading morning sunshine of each new day:
_____ _____ _____ _____

Your time zone is called _____. How far away from GMT is your time zone? _____

At the time you are in your geography class, what are people in Japan probably doing?

_____

GIS _____

Remote sensing _____

GPS _____

Mashup _____

What kind of technology helps us obtain GIS information? _____

What use does GPS have besides directions? _____

If you go to *Google Maps* and type in "Pizza" along with your zip code, you get a _____

Place _____

Toponym _____

Site _____

Situation _____

At right, draw a freehand road map from your house to school and label the two *locations,* along with a typonym, along the way:

Describe the *site* characteristics of this area you have drawn.

_____

_____

If you were giving directions to your house from school, what is one *situation* landmark or building you would use to help keep them on the right track?

_____

Region _____

Cultural landscape _____

Regional studies _____

Paul Vidal de la Blache _____

Jean Brunhes _____

Carl Sauer _____

Robert Platt _____

Formal region _____

Functional region _____

Vernacular region _____

Give an example of each:	Describe the two facets of culture:
FORMAL REGION	1)
FUNCTIONAL REGION	2)
VERNACULAR REGION	

Pg. 20   1 - BASIC CONCEPTS – Keys 3/4   Name _____

Remember- if you don't recycle the charade of life might be cut short by about 8 seconds at the very end

Globalization

Housing bubble

Transnational corporation

Headquarters

On this timeline, note at least three incidents on the road to the bursting of the housing bubble, which triggered the recession of 2008, in the order they happened:

2000   Today

Describe the connection between a transnational company and globalization:

Map 21: Why can *The North Face* be considered a transnational company?

While globalization may be good for economics, what are some negatives about it regarding culture?

Pic 21: Think of a cultural element that is local where you live (not McDonalds!) that reflects the globalization of culture:

Item: Reason:

Space

Distribution

Density

Concentration

Clustered vs. dispersed

Pattern

What is the distribution of houses in your neighborhood?
Can you sketch out your hood like in Pic 22? Try at right:

Pic 23: Circle the areas of the country with MLB teams:

1952		2013	
Northeast	Midwest	Northeast	Midwest
Mid-Atlantic	South	Mid-Atlantic	South
Great Plains	Rockies Mts.	Great Plains	Rockies Mts.
Southwest	Pacific	Southwest	Pacific

Sketch out the pattern below of the township and range system as in Chart 23 (bot.):

How does movement across space vary at your school? Note three patterns and times of day:

Behavioral geography

Humanistic geography

Poststructuralist geography

Connection

Hearth

Diffusion

Relocation diffusion

Expansion diffusion

Hierarchical diffusion

Contagious diffusion

Stimulus diffusion

Pic 26: Relocation diffusion: Circle the part of France that is least likely to be visited by foreigners: NW   NE
                                                                                                             SW   SE

Describe how a *hearth* emerges _____

_____

How many generations back did you have an ancestor who spoke a language other than English? 1= parents, 2=grandparents, 3=great grandparents, etc.:

_____

How is the spreading of a language from Europe to North America an example of relocation diffusion?

_____

Give an example of the following:

   hierarchical diffusion: *Contagious diffusion:*   *Stimulus diffusion:*

_____

Map 27: People in the Florida panhandle are more likely to be texting people in:

   Orlando, FL   *New Orleans, LA*   *Mobile, AL*

Distance decay _____

Space-time compression _____

Uneven development _____

It took Columbus _____ hours to cross the Atlantic, and Lindbergh _____ hours.

Estimate how many minutes it took John Glenn to cross the Atlantic.
Ask your math teacher for help if you can't figure it out.
Figure it out- remember, there are 24 time zones and the Atlantic is six.   _____ min.

Why is distance decay less of an issue now? | How would you contact someone on another
                                              | continent?
_____ |
                                              |_____
_____

How would you have done so in 1990? _____; In 1890? _____

If a corpo master in a Manhattan skyscraper calls the head of a factory in Guangzhou and orders an increase in the production of Robocop action figures, it is an example of

_____ diffusion because _____.

Resource _____

Renewable resource _____

Nonrenewable resource _____

Sustainability _____

Conservation _____

Preservation _____

Three pillars of sustainability _____

Biotic vs. abiotic _____

Atmosphere _____

Lithosphere _____

Hydrosphere _____

Biosphere _____

Pic 34: Describe where most earth life interacts: _____

Provide an example of an abiotic system that you personally interact with: _____

Climate _____

Climate types: _____

Monsoon _____

'Topos' _____

Ecosystem _____

Ecology _____

Erosion _____

Resource depletion _____

Cultural ecology _____

Carl Ritter _____

Environmental determinism _____

Alexander von Humboldt _____

Friedrich Ratzel _____

Ellen Churchill Semple _____

Ellsworth Huntington _____

Possibilism _____

Contrast *environmental determinism* and *possibilism*. Circle the word 'whereas' in your answer:

_____

_____

_____

_____

_____

_____

Polder _____

Dike _____

Zuider Zee _____

Everglades _____

Lake Okeechobee _____

How have humans altered the following places, and what is the book's tone, or point-of-view, on each activity:

   The Netherlands: *Florida:*

Alteration:

Author's tone:

Pg. 44   2 - POPULATION – Keys 1 & 2   Name _____
There are 7.3 gigahumans, so don't tell anyone they are "1 in a million." If they knew any math, they'd be insulted!

What is the environment of the Sahel region of West Africa like? | Mali has about 14 million people but is quite a large state. Why is it considered 'overpopulated?'

Demography _____

Overpopulation _____

Cartogram _____

Census _____

On the population cartogram, what are the ten 'big' countries containing over 100 million people?

_____

Circle the place with the higher population:

North America / Africa   Europe / Asia   Latin America / Oceania

How many siblings do you have? _____. How many did your mom have? _____.

How 'bout your dad? _____. How 'bout grandparents? _____ _____ _____ _____.

Describe any pattern you see: _____

Population cluster _____

Ecumene _____

Sparsely populated region _____

East Asia contains _____% of the world's population. Of what countries does it consist?

_____

South Asia contains _____% of the world's population. Of what countries does it consist?

_____

Southeast Asia contains _____% of the world's population. Name the *island countries* they live on:

What do dry lands, wet lands, cold lands and high lands have in common? _____

Arithmetic density _____

Physical density _____

Arable land _____

Agricultural density _____

Maps 48/49: Say you were putting together a recommendation for your government, which was trying to decide on how much food aid to provide to ten different countries. Would you use arithmetic density or physiological density to gauge the state of a country's relationship between land and people? Why?

_____

According to the agricultural density map, which two regions have the highest intensive use of their farmland?

North America   *Latin America*   *Europe*   *Africa*   *Asia*

CBR _____

CDR _____

NIR _____

Doubling time _____

Assuming the 21st century NIR of 1.2 percent keeps, what is   Will it be even across all countries?
The projected doubling time of the total world population?
                                                                 _____
_____   (MDC = developed country, LDC = developing country)

Of the natural increase rate, how much is in MDCs? _____, how about in LDCs? _____

The highest NIR is in _____, while _____ has a negative increase rate.

TFR _____

Mortality _____

Life expectancy _____

Infant mortality _____

Population pyramid _____

Dependency ratio

Sex ratio

Lawrence, KS has a lot of people in the _____ to _____ age group. Why is this so?

Name a city in your state that is likely to have   Why did you pick that city?
A similar population pyramid profile as Lawrence:

_____   _____

Why does Naples, FL have such a strangely shaped population pyramid?

The birthrate in Laredo, TX is significantly   *higher   lower*   than in the rest of the United States.

What does Rubenstein attribute this statistically different average birthrate to?

Many Asian countries have a distorted sex ratio in favor of males. Why is that?

Map 55 (bot.): List the sex ratio in the following places:

Place	*more men*	*more women*	*the same*
North America			
Latin America			
Western Europe			
Eastern Europe			
The Middle East			
Congo			
South Africa			
Indian Subcontinent			
China			
Australia			

Pg. 56 2 – POPULATION – Keys 3 & 4 Name _____

"Honey, let's move to a stage three society or higher." Huh?

Demographic transition _____

Demographic transition model _____

DTM stage 1 _____

DTM stage 2 _____

DTM stage 3 _____

DTM stage 4 _____

DTM stage 5 _____

Draw and label the X and Y-axes of the demographic model at right, stages 1-4 and from 0 to 60/1,000:

1) Draw the red and blue squiggles in stage 1. What causes this low growth pattern?

_____

_____

2) Draw the stage two's red and blue lines. What causes the population to go up in this stage?

_____

3) draw the stage three lines. The major change here is a declining birth rate- what social factors cause this?

_____

_____

4) Draw stage four's connection between birth and death rate. What is the general level of wealth and quality of life in countries in stage 4?

_____

If you were going to start a business taking care of elderly people, you be do best to open your retirement home in:

Cape Verde   *Denmark*   *Chile*

Where would you do best to open a childcare facility?   *Cape Verde   Denmark   Chile*

Agricultural revolution

Industrial revolution

Medical revolution

ZPG

Women's education factor

Health care factor

Contraception

Why are the following said to lower birth rates?

Education   *Health Care*   *Contraception*

Why has Bangladesh struggled with keeping birthrates low?	Some reasons Sub-Saharan Africa struggles with keeping birthrates low are:
_____	_____
_____	_____
_____	_____

The major form of family planning in Germany, which has a negative birth rate, is:	The major form(s) of family planning in China, which has a low birth rate, is:
_____	_____

The percentage of people in Nigeria *not* using family planning is about _____ percent.

Thomas Malthus

Neo-Malthusians

Summarize how Thomas Malthus saw the relationship between people and resources:

What do neo-Malthusians argue- how is it similar and different to what Malthus argued back then?

Similarities	Differences

Identify some faults Malthus' critics find in his doomsday theory:

_____

_____

While the doomsday scenario didn't come to pass in Britain, it did on Easter Island, where the Polynesian settlers of the island cut down all the trees over many centuries and did not replant them. Their society collapsed, and when Capt. Cook found them in the 18th century, they were warring over the last bits of food. Britain and Easter Island present us with two stark paths. Which path do you think *Earth* will take in the 21st century, based on the charts in the chapter? Why?

_____

_____

Negative birthrate _____

Family planning _____

Forced sterilization _____

Family welfare _____

One Child Policy _____

Abortion _____

Infanticide _____

Pro-natalist policy _____

As Japan faces a shortage of young workers and a top-heavy population pyramid, and immigration to Japan is very tightly controlled, what 'stark choice' are young Japanese women having to make?

_____

Some countries are entering a new "5th stage", characterized by a negative birth rate. Go back to the map on pg. 51 and look at countries "under zero." Name three places who are candidates for the new stage 5 of the DTM:

In contrast to the rest of the world, Europe faces an   *overpopulation*   *underpopulation*   crisis.

Add the 5th stage to your chart on the other side. What happens in this stage with the birth and death rate lines?

___

Compare the population policies of the two largest countries in the world:

INDIA   *CHINA*

Epidemiologic transition

ET stage 1

ET stage 2

ET stage 3

ET stage 4

Pandemic

Cholera

Dr. John Snow

EPIDEMIOLOGIC TRANSITION STAGE	**CHARACTERISTICS**
1	
2	
3	
4	
5?	

According to the map on pg. 65, name 10 countries reporting Cholera outbreaks:

1	2	3	4	5
6	7	8	9	10

The reasons for a stage 5 are disputed. Summarize the three options, and rate them 1-3 as the one that is most sensible to you.

        EVOLUTION   *POVERTY*   *CONNECTIONS*

My rating: _____

*Go to AidsVu.org/map to see the infection rate in your county.

Infectious diseases _____

Malaria _____

DDT-resistant mosquito _____

TB _____

Swine flu/SARS _____

HIV/AIDS _____

How did AIDS reach the USA and what kind of diffusion is that?

_____

Name ten countries with an infant mortality rate of above 60 deaths per 1,000 births:

1 _____ 2 _____ 3 _____ 4 _____ 5 _____

6 _____ 7 _____ 8 _____ 9 _____ 10 _____

What average life expectancy does an average person in each world region have these days?

North America _____   **Middle East** _____   **East Asia** _____

Latin America _____   **South Asia** _____   **Southeast Asia** _____

Europe _____   **Russia** _____   **Australia/NZ** _____

Aside from Sub-Saharan Africa, what other large *country* has over 25% of kids w/out measles immunization? -----------------------------------

The world region with the lowest number of physicians (doctors) per person is _____

Pg. 77   3 - MIGRATION – Keys 1 & 2   Name _____

You planning on spending the rest of your life in this room?

Preview: What are the migrants in Dubai on Pg. 76 lining up for? _____

What flag do the people watching a parade in NY have? _____

What do the men in the boat heading for Italy want? _____

Migration _____

Circulation _____

Immigration _____

Emigration _____

E.G. Ravenstein _____

Ravenstein's laws _____

Wilbur Zelinsky _____

Migration transition _____

Three main reasons people migrate- their objectives- are:

1   2   3

Ravenstein's laws of migration are:

1

2

3

In Zelinsky's migration transition, what happens to the migration patterns in a society as it become more advanced in stage 3 and 4?

International migration _____

Voluntary migration _____

Forced migration _____

Internal migration

Interregional migration

Intraregional migration

Map 80. If a Mexican were moving *within* Mexico, what might their likely destination be? _____

One-fourth of Mexicans have now migrated - at least temporarily- to the United States. According to the map, who migrates *into* Mexico?

_____

Of those migrants into Mexico from the south, their likely destination, according to the map, is:

    Mexico   United States

How many times have *you* moved in your life? _____. From where to where?

_____

_____

If you know the motivation for moving, what was it?

_____

The three largest migration flows are:

1   2   3

_____

Map 81: Continents where there is very little out-migration are:

1   2

Continents where there is little in-migration are:

1   2

Europe doesn't count because some people move out to this area:

_____

Asia doesn't count for 'only a little in-migration, because some people move to Asia from this region:

_____

Chart 82: If you put your finger over "1960," what do you notice about immigration to the USA?

Before 1960: _____

After 1960: _____

Chart 82: Sketch out the graphic:

10

8

6

4

2

0

1860   1900   1920   1940   1960   1980   2000 2010

List the national origins of people coming to America during the following eras:

1607-1840　　　*1840-1890*　　　*1890-1965*　　　*1965-Today*

The states with the most immigrants living there are the following five:

1　　　2　　　3　　　4　　　5

What changed in the general direction Americans were moving around 1950?
Hint: Invention of A/C had something to do with it!

Summarize the reason and times for each phase of American interregional migration:

Pattern	**Era**	**Reasons**
Hugging coast:		
Crossing Appalachians:		
Rushing to Gold:		
Filling in Great Plains:		
Moving South:		

Center of population gravity

Do the same thing for Russians' interregional migration:

Pattern	Era	Reasons

Which tribe was removed to Indian Territory by boat? _____

What modern state is what was formerly known as 'Indian Territory'? _____

Do the same thing for the following interregional migration:

Place	Pattern	Era	Reasons
Canada			
China			
Brazil			

What kinds of things prompt people to *intraregionally* migrate from rural to urban areas?

What kinds of things prompt people to *intraregionally* migrate from urban to suburban areas?

What kinds of things prompt people to *intraregionally* migrate from urban to rural areas?

List the six ways of *intraregionally* migrating in order of how many people did that in 2010:

1   2

3   4

5   6

Map 91: Locate your state. Does it have a net in or out migration? _____

Map 91: Locate your county. Does it have a net in or out migration? _____

Do you plan on migrating anywhere after high school/college? Characterize it using the descriptive terms from the section:

Pg. 92   3 - MIGRATION – Keys 3 & 4   Name _____

Taking Human Geography is your birthright. That being said, get working!

Push factor _____

Pull factor _____

Refugee _____

UNHCR _____

IDP _____

Asylum seeker _____

Floodplain _____

If you are a person who writes an application to a country which is not your own to let you in and give you shelter from people or disaster within your country, you are considered

_____

If your house is flooded and you are relocated to another city, you are considered a

_____

Of all elderly Americans who move to a new place, how many chose Florida? _____

In the Sehel, where to people who have nothing and are displaced because of lack of water go? _____

Guest workers _____

If migrant workers in Europe wind up with low skill, low paying jobs, why would they migrate to Europe?

_____

The terrible toll of WWII on young men [workers] in Europe caused German and other leaders to

offer _____ programs to help rebuild the economic base.

Where do workers travel in the following places:

　　　CHINA　　　　　　　　　　　　　*SOUTHEAST ASIA*

_____

Pic 96: Is the backup heavier on the U.S. to Mexico side, or the Mexico to U.S. side? Why?

Intervening obstacle

1924 Immigration Act (Johnson-Reed Act)

1965 Immigration Act (Hart-Cellar Act)

1978 quota

1990 quota

Family reunification quota

Skilled workers quota

Diversity quota

Brain drain

Ellis Island

Of the following acts, which do you think was the best immigration system for the U.S.?

1924   1965   1978   1990

Illegal immigrant

Immigration concerns:

Sanctuary city

Unauthorized immigrant

Undocumented immigrant

Illegal alien

Is it morally acceptable to allow most doctors and engineers from poorer countries to immigrate to more advanced nations? If you were a lawyer arguing for and then against the system, what would your main points be?

FOR BRAIN DRAIN	**AGAINST BRAIN DRAIN**

If chain migration can bring in an unlimited number of people over time because everyone is related to someone else, and those others are related to still others, if you were a lawyer arguing for or against keeping this policy, what would your main points be?

FOR CHAIN MIGRATION	AGAINST CHAIN MIGRATION

What was the outcome of the Ellis Island dispute and what economic consequences did it have?

The source country for most unauthorized immigrants is _____.

The USA is the only country in the world that gives automatic citizenship to anyone born the U.S., after a judicial ruling in 1980 interpreted the Fourteenth Amendment to include children of illegal migrants as American citizens- even if the parents are not American. If you were a lawyer arguing whether this was a good or problematic policy, discuss your main points:

FOR BIRTHRIGHT CITIZENSHIP	AGAINST BIRTHRIGHT CITIZENSHIP

Why might Texas and California have the highest numbers of unauthorized immigrants but Nevada has the highest *percentage?*

Map 99: Draw the USA/Mexico border as a line, noting U.S. states and Mexican stats, and cities 'twinned' with San Diego, Calexico, Nogales, Douglas, El Paso, Presidio, Eagle Pass, Laredo, Progreso and Brownsville:

Why do Americans and Europeans have concerns about current immigration patterns?

What is the default American feeling toward the following illegal immigration-related item:

BORDER PATROLS   *WORKPLACE*   *CIVIL RIGHTS*   *LOCAL INITIATIVES*

What was the controversial law passed in 2010 by Arizona? What happened to the law in 2012?

Should a state be able to make its own immigration-related laws? If you were a lawyer arguing for and then against the right of Arizona to allow its police to ask people about their citizenship, what would your main points be?

FOR STATES' RIGHTS   **AGAINST STATES' RIGHTS**

What is a 'sanctuary city?' _____

Migrating from one country to another in Europe has become **easier   harder**   for *Europeans.*

Migrating from Africa or Asia to Europe had become **easier   harder**   than in the past.

Schengen Treaty

Pic 103: What do you think the word *'Regularisez'* means in the context of pro-immigration rally in France? What might *'Incontrolee'* mean in context at bottom?

REGULARISEZ   **INCONTROLEE**

Since up to a million Syrian and other refugees streamed into Europe in 2015, immigration and its limits has become the biggest issue of the day. Hungary built a fence to try to stop them, while Germany and Sweden invited them to settle there. Overall, Europe has a negative birthrate yet a high standard of living. If you were a lawyer arguing for and then against the right of people to illegally immigrate to Europe to fill in the missing people, what would be your main points?

FOR MORE IMMIGRATION   **AGAINST MORE IMMIGRATION**

Pg. 107   4 – FOLK AND POP CULTURE – Keys 1/2   Name _____
Prepare for Culture Shock!

Pic 107: Are the people with the lamas- or the dancers- at right posing for money? | Who is their target audience?

Folk culture _____

Popular culture _____

Habit _____

Custom _____

Pic 109: Why are these roots considered part of *material* culture? _____   List some items of material Culture that you own: _____

Which is personal: *habit   custom*   Which is collective: *habit   custom*

Think of two habits you perform daily: _____

Think of two customs people in a collective that you are a part of have:

_____

If you add up all of a group's customs, you have the core aspect of that group's _____

Pic 109: The Chrysler President's _____ of wearing sweaters breaks the _____ of his pals. Before 1900 there was little _____ culture. Peoples had their own _____ culture.

Hearth _____

Diffusion _____

Distribution _____

Folk music _____

Musical meccas _____

Pic 110: What city might lay claim to being the hearth of popular culture? _____

Name 3 examples of pop culture music:

Provide 3 examples of pop culture fashion:

Submit 3 examples of pop culture foods:

Describe technology's role in mutating aspects of folk culture into a universalistic popular culture:

It is a *coincidence* that the invention of radio, faster transportation happened at the same time as the beginning of pop culture:

          True   *False*

Pic 111 (bot.): Four religious groups in the Himalaya Mountains are:

1   2   3   4

What geographic factors might account for why there is so much cultural diversity in such a small area?

Folk music tends to be: *organic and homespun*   *commercialized and universalistic*

Maps 113: Draw the basic outlines of the two 'maps' of pop music:

AT&T/Yifan Hu map: London Subway map:

Draw lines matching the cultural hearths with the genre of music:

New York   *Detroit*   *Nashville*   *New Orleans*   *Vienna*

Country   *Dixieland Jazz*   *Motown*   *Classical*   *Hip hop*

Soccer's hearth _____

Association football _____

Folk sports _____

In medieval _____, football (soccer) began as a folk custom of village rivalry.

Relate how soccer diffused to be the most popular sport in the entire world:

To Holland _____

To Spain _____

To Russia _____

To Globe _____

The Olympics originated from this hearth in ancient times: _____

Relate the local hearths of the following sports, and indicate where they have diffused:

    CRICKET   WUSHU   BASEBALL

Folk clothing

Burqa

Provide some specific examples of folk clothing and popular clothing styles:

    FOLK   POPULAR

Give an example of something you would wear to school that would be 'weird' from a folk culture:	Where in the world might you be uncomfortable wearing what you are wearing now?

Folk cuisines

Terroir

Bostan

Taboo

Kosher

Halal

Vineyard

Wine and Christianity

Wine and Islam

What kind of folk foods do bostans in Istanbul, Turkey provide for the people growing them?

There are many famous food taboos in the world - things allowed in one culture are not okay everywhere. Name a taboo food in the following cultures:

Jewish (Kosher menu):

Muslim (Halal menu):

American:

Hindu:

You personally:

Think of some ethnic restaurants you have been, such as Greek, Mexican, Italian, Chinese, etc. What kind of foods did you find there? To what extent do you think it is original to the place and to what extent do you think it was "Americanized" i.e.: Tex-Mex, or NY style Chinese... .

Food: Extent:

Why is cola considered a popular culture food?

Place the country next to which brand is dominant there: *Canada, USA, Mexico, Brazil, France, South Africa, Saudi Arabia, Russia, India, Thailand, Vietnam, Japan, Australia*

Coke:

Pepsi:

Some countries favor one for political reasons, which may seem strange for you. Why do they like...

Pepsi in Quebec: _____

Coke in Russia: _____

Pepsi in Muslim countries: _____

Utah and Nevada have differing levels of alcohol consumption per capita (per person). Why?

Think of a product popular in your state that is also made from what is grown in your state:

| Why do France, Spain and Italy produce more wine than Norway, Sweden and Poland?

Why might South Africa, Australia and New Zealand produce more wine than Libya, Iraq and Indonesia?

Wood housing

Brick housing

Kashgar style

Turpan style

Yinchuan style

Dunhuang style

Middle Atlantic style

Lower Chesapeake style

New England style

Modern styles (5)

Neo-Eclectic styles (4)

Bungalow

Double pile

Single pile

Irregular massed

Ranch

Folk housing. Brunhes said the house means a lot in the world. You can "tell" where you are because we use the materials around us, plus our culture and skills to build the houses for ourselves is always a bit unique. What are the most common building materials for houses?

Where is mud-brick used?

Why does McColl think the houses in central and western Chinese cities along the Silk Road differ?

_____

The three hearths of US folk housing are:

1

2

3

What kind of house do you live in- which type is it most similar to? _____

Draw as best you can and label the 14 kinds of house style (add mobile home if you want!):

1	2	3	4	5
6	7	8	9	10
11	12	13	14	15?

Got a favorite? What style do you think YOU would want in the future? _____

Pg. 126   4 – FOLK AND POP CULTURE – Keys 3/4   Name _____

What if you wake up one day and that filter the school has blocking bad sites on the Internet was everywhere?

      Good   *Bad*   *Both*

TV and leisure

TV diffusion

Not everyone in the world has access to popular culture. What are the main reasons some don't?

_____

The most popular activity in the world is _____. World average is _____ hrs./day.

In USA, average is _____ hrs./day. Are you above or below the world/USA averages? _____

In 1954, the country with the most TVs per person was _____

What regions of the world did TV diffuse to the most by 1970? _____

Three countries with less than 1 TV per 1,000 people in 2005 are _____

The first experimental TV broadcasts were from the _____ Olympics in _____

Contrast American men and women's weekend habits:

      MEN   **WOMEN**

Pie Chart 127: On the left below, draw the chart. Then on the right, draw *your* chart for your weekends with the same categories- and be honest ☺

      AVG.   **ME**

Internet diffusion

Facebook

Twitter

Youtube

What similarities and differences do you see between the diffusion of TV and of the Internet?

SIMILARITIES	DIFFERENCES

Look at the key on the Facebook, Twitter and Youtube maps. Why is the FB map not effective in communicating comparisons between large countries like India with small ones like Belgium?

Why does popular culture 'threaten' local folk cultures around the world?

Some countries have laws that say a certain percentage of programming (radio, TV, etc.) have to be local, or else, native to that country. For example, in France there is a minimum quota for French language shows so the market is not dominated by Hollywood and other U.S. or British shows. If you were a lawyer arguing for or against this policy, what would be your main points?

FOR LAWS TO BENEFIT LOCAL PROGRAMS	FOR A FREE MARKET APPROACH

Entertainment

Cultural imperialism

Media news bias

1984

Why is popular culture considered by some to be a form of cultural imperialism (domination)?

The U.S. entertainment industry is famous for 'pushing the envelope' toward edgy content. Iranian leader Ayatollah Khomeini famously called the United States "The Great Satan" because of what he believed were negative messages in this kind of U.S. pop culture. What are some things countries do to help prevent popular culture from 'invading' their cultural space?

_____

In places like North Korea and China, the government has virtually 100% control over TV and radio content. In Russia, the government retains some control. Some have accused these policies of putting a pro-government bias in the news in those countries. However, what have these governments turned around and claimed about Western media that claims to be 'free and unbiased?'

_____

Give examples why countries limit access to each type of website:

POLITICAL CONTENT   **SOCIAL CONTENT**   **CONFLICT/SECURITY**   **INTERNET TOOLS**

Countries
_____

Examples
_____

Amish
_____

Jakob Ammonn
_____

Sex tourism
_____

Dowry killings
_____

Landscape pollution
_____

Uniformity
_____

Recycling
_____

How have the Amish fought to keep their folk culture alive?

_____

(Whatever you do, don't Youtube: Weird Al Amish Paradise)

How has Western culture changed traditional Indian approaches to marriage and women's roles? Explain how women are using technology to change Indian culture:

Is the landscape around where you live uniform in the way explained on pg. 134? How so? Or if not, why not?

_____

_____

In what ways is golf folk culture...   ...and pop culture

_____

In the USA, _____ million of the _____ million tons of garbage was recycled.

How much more or less trash went into the landfills in 2010 than in 1990? _____

Pg. 137. Sketch out the trash cans below:

Items recycled a lot   **Items not recycled very much**

_____

What do you commonly recycle at home?   At school?

_____

Recycling is almost always voluntary. If you were a lawyer asked to present a case on making recycling a LAW, punishable by fines and imprisonment (after a 3rd offense), what would be your arguments for and against:

      FOR RECYCLING LAWS   **AGAINST RECYCLING LAWS**

_____

Pg. 143   5 – LANGUAGE – Key Issues 1/2   NAME _____
What did you say? What did you say to me?

Language _____

Literary tradition _____

Official language _____

Language family _____

Language branch _____

Language group _____

Dutch kids, who live in the country _____, learn _____ languages in high school.

How many languages do you know: Fluently _____ Partially _____ Taking it now _____

What does it mean to say that some languages have a 'literary tradition?'

_____

What century did English diffuse to North America? _____ How 'bout the Philippines? _____

There are _____ languages with over 100,000,000 speakers

There are _____ languages with ten to a hundred million speakers

There are _____ languages with one to ten million speakers

_____

Draw the best graphic in this chapter, the *Big Language Tree* on pg. 145. Draw everything above the line, but not below, so you'll have 13 starting points at the bottom. Now go ahead, we'll wait ☺

Indo-European

Sino-Tibetan

Mandarin

Other Chinese (7)

Logograms

Circle: In   *China*   *India*   there is a relatively small number of languages, which is considered a source of national strength and unity.

Pic 147: Draw one of the Chinese logograms, pick whichever you want:

Summarize the following for each language
family, for notes, write whatever you think
seems suspiciously like a future test question:

FAMILY	NUMBER	PLACE/EXAMPLES	NOTES
AUSTRONESIAN			
AUSTRO-ASIATIC			
TAI KADAI			
JAPANESE			
KOREAN			
AFRO-ASIATIC			
ALTAIC			
URALIC			
NIGER-CONGO			
NILO-SAHARAN			

KHOISAN

INDO-EUROPEAN LANGUAGE BRANCHES: LIST LANGUAGES IN EACH BRANCH

GERMANIC   *ROMANCE*   *BALTO-SLAVIC*   *OTHER*

FAMILY	**NUMBER**	**PLACE/EXAMPLES**	**NOTES**
GERMANIC			
INDIC			
IRANIAN			
EAST SLAVIC			
BALTIC			
WEST SLAVIC			
SOUTH SLAVIC			
ROMANCE			

Angles

1066

1607

1620

Three German tribes moved to England around 450 A.D. They were:

1   2   3

Trace the etymology of "England" _____
                                 (*Wow you got a new angle in thinking about languages now!*)

Why does English have a lot of French/Latin based words in it too?

List 4 words with their German and Romance (French) equivalents:

1)   2)

3)   4)

Summarize how English diffused to North America:	*When and how did Romance languages diffuse?*

PIE

Nomadic warrior hypothesis

Sedentary farmer hypothesis

Kurgan vs. Anatolian theory

Why do linguists believe Proto-Indo-European speakers lived in a cold climate but without ocean access?

Which seems more likely to you, the Nomadic Warrior or Sedentary Farmer Hypothesis? Why?

Pg. 158 — 5 – LANGUAGE – Key Issues 3/4 — NAME _____

Dialect _____

Isogloss _____

Colonial speech areas (3) _____

Soft drink dialects _____

Pic 158: In the Eastern USA, summarize the three dialect regions and note what makes them different:

NEW ENGLAND	SOUTHEASTERN	MIDLANDS

Map 159: What dialect of English is most prevalent in your area _____

How do most people in your county refer to a 'soft drink'
_____

What are some other ways people refer to soft drinks?
_____

Standard language _____

RP _____

British vs. American English _____

Noah Webster _____

Broadcasters on British TV use this dialect
_____

Why don't Americans speak RP?
_____

Why is English vocabulary different in North America?

What was Noah Webster's contribution?

Write a quick sentence containing five words in the American dialect of English automobile-related terms in the upper right:

_____

_____

Now write that same sentence, but substitute the American terms for British terms.

_____

Would you understand someone if they asked you that?   Yes   No   *If they repeated it*

Castilian Spanish _____

Treaty of Tordesillas _____

Catalan _____

Creole _____

What region of Spain does standard Spanish come from? _____

Who decides what 'official Spanish' is, and how do they meet?	Why might tourists from Spain have a hard time understanding Peruvian Spanish as time goes on?

Summarize the linguistic issues highlighted in the chapter related to the following places:

ITALY	**GALICIA**	**MOLDOVA**	**CREOLES**

Summarize the languages and issues involved in the following multilingual states:

BELGIUM	**SWITZERLAND**	**NIGERIA**

Isolated language _____

Basque

Extinct language

Basque is the only language in Europe that _____

Why does Icelandic change so slowly compared with other languages?

If the students in your school spoke a unique language that only you knew, would you have more or fewer speakers of that language than the language Koro Aka from India?
_____

Small tribes that were always previously isolated are now integrated with other tribes around them or otherwise part of a larger community. Do their tribal languages always survive?
        Y   N

Out of the 500 languages of the Peruvian tribes found by the Spanish, _____ of their languages survive in the present day.

Why is Gothic a dead language? _____

What were some difficulties about reviving Hebrew as a language?

Endangered language

Celtic

Aborigines

List some ways the different Celtic languages are being preserved by their former speakers:

| *WELSH* | *IRISH* | *BRETON* | *SCOTTISH* | *CORNISH* |

Lingua Franca

International language

What historical events led to English becoming the primary language in Australia and New Zealand, literally on the other side of the world from England?

The White Australia policy **encouraged   discouraged**   Asian immigration in the 20th century.

How is New Zealand's language policy different than that of Australia?
Which policy do you prefer and why?

_____

How has the French government encouraged the preservation of little used languages?

_____

What historical trends might account for so many countries in the world having English as their official or de-facto official language?

_____

What language do pilots speak in to foreign air traffic controllers? _____

What language do Swiss bankers speak with their foreign clients? _____

Europeans didn't always use English as the language of cross-cultural communication. What language did they use for that in the 19th century? Hint: the term lingua-franca gives it away!

_____

Before that, what language was used? Hint: its 1) the language of the old Roman Empire, 2) the language of the Catholic Church, and 3) the language of scientific nomenclature

_____

Is it more likely that: _____
    a. Toyota will send an English-speaking employee to the USA to deal with Americans.
    b. General Motors will send a Japanese-speaking employee to Japan to deal with Japanese.

Diffusion of English

Pidgin

Appalachian English

While English diffused through relocation centuries ago, how does it diffuse today and why?

_____

What are some ways Ebonics is different than standard American English:

_____

Why are the French mad at some innocent little ol' English words?

_____

Give an example of the ways in which the following combine with English:

FRANGLAIS   SPANGLISH   DENGLISH

What trends does Rubenstein discuss related to the status and future prospects of the following:

SPANISH IN THE UNITED STATES   FRENCH IN CANADA

How has the arrival of the Internet in the 1990s affected the use of English?

If you have a phone or computer, go to Google.fr   what language is it? _____

Now go to Google.ru   what language is it? _____

Now go to Google.cn   what language is it? _____

Now go to Google.es   what language is it? _____

Why was there controversy when Google China came out?

Go to Wikipedia.org. It always notes the top 10 "Wikipedia languages", meaning the ones with the most articles written in that language by users. What are the top 10 now?

Language	# Articles	Language	# Articles
1		2	
3		4	
5		6	
7		8	
9		10	

Any surprises?

Pg. 182	6 – RELIGION – Key Issue 1/2	Name_____
Hey so what's the etymology of your eschatology?

Yellow Page: Key Issue 1 describes _____ religions are distributed.

What does Key Issue 2 describe? _____

K.I. 3 discusses: _____

K.I. 4 examines: _____

Dalai Lama _____

Tibet / Xizang _____

The Dalai Lama is the religious leader of a _____ sect in Tibet.

The capital of Tibet is, or rather was, _____, in the _____ Mts.

After China invaded Tibet in _____, they turned it into the province of _____.

Was the Chinese communist government religiously tolerant to Tibetans?   Y   N

What are some things the Chinese government had done for Tibet that:

BRING MODERN CONVENIENCES	SECURE ITS HOLD ON THE PROVINCE

Ethnic religion _____

Universalizing religion _____

Atheism _____

Agnosticism _____

Map 185: State the major religion of the following regions. If it's a mix, put 'mix':

North America:	North Africa:	South Asia:
Latin America:	Middle East:	East Asia:
Europe:	Central Asia:	SE Asia:
Russia:	Sub-Saharan Africa:	Oceania:

What is the difference between atheism and agnosticism?

___

Rank the following in size, from trunk of the tree to twig: *branch, denomination, religion, sect*

| 1 | 2 | 3 | 4 |

Branch

Denomination

Christianity

Catholic Christian

Protestant Christian

Orthodox Christian

Isolated churches

Graph 184 (World)-187 (USA): Note the estimated percentage of U.S. believers in the following denominations:

Catholic _____	*Lutheran* _____	*Episcopalian* _____
Baptist _____	*Mormon/LDS* _____	*Reformed* _____
Not religious _____	*Presbyterian* _____	*Muslim* _____
Methodist _____	*Orthodox* _____	*Hindu* _____
Pentecostal _____	*Jewish* _____	*Buddhist* _____
		Jeh. Witness _____

Contrast: ***Ethnic Religion***   ***Universalizing Religion***

___

***Britannica* says the percentages of Christians who are in each branch worldwide is:**

Catholic   ***Protestant***   ***Orthodox***

The self-governing Eastern Orthodox churches are in the following countries:

___

Two small Christian churches in northeast Africa are the _____

How was the early Armenian Church important? _____

The conflict over Nagorno-Karabakh is between _____ and _____

Lebanese Christians are generally part of the _____ sect.

Utah is home to this sect of Christians _____.

Islam

Sunni Muslim

Shi'a Muslim

Black Muslim/Nation of Islam

Islam is associated with the Middle East but half of Muslims live outside it. Where?

1   2   3   4

The percentage of Sunni Muslims is _____, while _____% are Shi'ite.

Five majority Shi'ite countries are:

1   2   3   4   5

Since the 1960s, c. 20 million Muslims have migrated to Europe. What is the current situation of Islam on the European and North American cultural landscape? _____

While most American Muslims immigrated to the U.S. starting around 1980, a homegrown group called the Black Muslims started earlier. What is their story? _____

Rank the three branches of Buddhism by number of followers:

1   2   3

Explain why it is more difficult to count the number of Buddhists in the world than most other belief systems:

Theravada

Mahayana

Vajrayana

Sikhism

Baha'i

Two other universalizing religions are _____ and _____.

Which one is based in India? _____. What are its major beliefs?

_____

What are the major beliefs of the other one?

_____

Hinduism

Vaishnavism

Sivaism

Syncretism

Confucianism

Taoism

Shamanism

Paganism

Juchte

Animism

Spiritism

Judaism

Monotheism

Polytheism

Abraham

Jesus _____

Muhammad _____

Hinduism, Judaism and others are considered 'ethnic' religions, why?
_____

Most Hindus live in _____. Where do the rest live? _____

Siddhartha Gautama _____

Buddhism _____

4 Noble Truths _____

Gospels _____

Messiah _____

Last Supper _____

Resurrection _____

Salvation _____

Pope _____

Baptism _____

Confirmation _____

Eucharist _____

Penance _____

Matrimony _____

Holy Orders _____

Anointment of the Sick _____

1054 Split _____

Patriarch _____

1517 Reformation _____

Martin Luther (95 Theses) _____

Personal salvation

The basic story of the Buddha's process of Enlightenment is that he:

Buddhism is based on Siddhartha Gautama's Four Noble Truths- summarize them briefly:

1

2

3

4

The basic Christian belief is that Jesus came as the long-awaited _____ to bring the news of heaven's existence to the people and sacrifice himself for the original sin of humanity, redeeming them, and thereby placing their moral lives- and their salvation- into their own hands.

How are Catholics different than other Christians?

The Orthodox-Catholic split occurred in _____, while the Catholic-Protestant split happened in _____

Five Pillars

Shahadah

Salat

Zakat

Ramadan

Hajj

Sarah / Hagar

Isaac / Ismail

622 Hijra

Caliph

Shah

Ayatollah

Guru Nanak _____

Guru Granth Sahib _____

Aryans _____

Dravidians _____

Complete the chart:

                / +Sarah = Isaac, patriarch in _____ and _____.

    Abraham—

               \ +Hagar = Ishmael, patriarch in _____.

Relate the key incidents in the story of Muhammad's revelation of Islam:

_____

_____

The Sikhs originated in _____ around 500 years ago.

Why are the origins of Hinduism unknown? _____

Diffusion of Christianity _____

Constantine _____

Theodosius _____

Paul _____

Missionaries _____

Mormons _____

Diffusion of Islam _____

Relate four explanations for the successful diffusion of Christianity:

1

2

3

4

Relate three explanations for the successful diffusion of Islam:

1

2

3

Relate two reasons for the successful diffusion of Buddhism:

1

2

Diffusion of Buddhism	
Shintoism	
Mauritius	
Diaspora	
Ghettos	

Religions can blend when peoples mingle their belief systems. Find four times it happened:

	Blending Religions	*Location and Description*
1		
2		
3		
4		

Ethnic religions diffuse differently. Judaism's diffusion can be characterized like this (hint: use and define the word 'diaspora'):

Draw the pie-charts on Jewish settlement and conclude some reasons Jews have migrated to the places they did:

Pg. 200   6 – RELIGION – Key Issue ¾   Name_____
                Why does existence exist?

Sacred space _____

Church _____

Mosque _____

Minaret _____

Muezzin _____

Pagoda _____

Place of Worship _____

Golden Temple _____

For what reasons does a Christian church specifically play a critical role in the organization of space? What symbols does it have in its architecture?

_____

_____

What are some unique designs in churches in different parts of the United States?

_____

A Muslim mosque has a different significance than a Christian church- why?

_____

Name three features of a typical mosque:

1   2   3

_____

Name three features of a typical Hindu temple:

1   2   3

_____

How do Hindu temples and Buddhist pagodas differ in religious purpose?

_____

What role did the idea of 'pilgrimage' take in the placement decisions of pagodas? Why are Baha'i temples located where they are?

Pagodas	**Baha'i temple**

Pilgrimage

Shrine

Mecca

Ka'ba

How is a pilgrimage different than a 'vacation'?

Name some holy pilgrimage sites for the following religions:

BUDDHIST   *ISLAMIC*

SIKH   *HINDU*

CHRISTIAN   *JEWISH*

Tirtha

Ganges river

Cosmogony

Solstice

Pick two religions and relate how their cosmogonies differs:

#1   #2

Catacombs

Cremation

Tower of Silence _____

Exposure _____

Utopian settlement _____

Commons _____

Toponyms _____

How do each of the following dispose with the bodies of people who have died?

Christians   *Hindus*   *Zoroastrians*   *Micronesians*

Why is Salt Lake City, Utah a good example of a utopian settlement?

_____

Passover _____

Sukkot _____

Shavuot _____

Rosh Hashanah _____

Yom Kippur _____

Lunar calendar _____

Easter _____

Christmas _____

Jewish holidays tend to be based on:

_____

Why are solstices important in calendars? How many are there per year?

_____

While both Jews and Muslims use the lunar calendar, discuss the differences in the way they use it:

Jews: *Muslims:*

Why do Christian branches celebrate Easter Sunday on different days?

What does the Easter holiday commemorate?

Hierarchical religion

Bishop of Rome

Archbishop

Bishop

Priest

Autonomous religion

Roman Catholic Christianity is a good example of a (circle): *hierarchical   autonomous*   structure.

Why are dioceses in Latin America larger than those in Europe?

Based on the map, 5 cities that serve as bishoprics are: 1   2

3   4   5

Is Islam also hierarchical? _____. What is the only formal organization of territory in Islam?

If you get down to the fundamentals of anything, what are you in effect doing?

Fundamentalism

Taliban

Graven image

Quran

Caste

Brahmans

Kshatriyas

Vaisyas _____

Sudras _____

Dalits _____

Why is fundamentalism increasing? _____

Why did Taliban fundamentalism and modern culture clash?

What aspects of Hinduism clash with modern culture? _____

"Opium of the masses" _____

Communism _____

Religious revival _____

Khmer Rouge _____

IRA / UDF _____

What was Czar Peter I the Great's relationship with the Orthodox Christian church in Russia in the 18th century, compared with the relationship the communist leaders of the 20th century had with the church?

_____

_____

What effect did the following have on Buddhism in Indochina (Southeast Asia):

a) Vietnam War **b) Communist takeover**

_____

What was the argument about during the following religious conflicts:

a) Ireland **b) The Crusades**

_____

Promised Land _____

Crusades _____

Partition of Palestine Mandate _____

Jerusalem

1948 Independence war

1956 Suez war

1967 Six Day war

1973 Yom Kippur war

Camp David Accords

Categorize the following terms into two categories of four:

Arab, Islam, Israeli, Jew, Muslim, Palestinian, Refugee, Zionism

_____ _____ _____ _____

_____ _____ _____ _____

Palestinian perspectives

PLO

West Bank

Gaza Strip

West Bank Barrier

Summarize the history of the modern Arab-Israeli conflict in timeline form:

Why is Israel building the West Bank partition wall? _____

Israeli perspectives

Temple of Solomon

Second Temple (Herod)

Dome of the Rock

On pg. 221, what is the significance of the following religious places:

WESTERN WALL   *DOME OF THE ROCK*

Samuel Huntington developed a 'Clash of Civilizations' world map, and identified religious boundaries between civilizations as some of the most violent. On the other hand, in communist countries that atheistic governments ran, millions were rounded up into prisons and killed. What do you think is to blame for man's inhumanity to man?

Pg. 227   7 – ETHNICITY - Key Issue 1/2   Name_____

Got one?

Ethnicity _____

Race _____

Racism _____

Racist _____

What nationality do you identify with? _____. What ethnicity? _____

How is race different than ethnicity?	What are some features of biological race?

Why is skin color something of interest to geographers?	What does a 'racist' believe about race?

Why does Barack Obama illustrate the complexity of designating race/ethnicity?

1

2

3

4

Hispanic _____

Latino/Latina _____

African American _____

Black _____

Mixed race _____

Ethnic clustering: state scale _____

Asian American

Note the 19 choices (20 if you include 'Hispanic or non-Hispanic') the U.S. Census gives for people to choose from when answering the question on what race they are:

If you were answering the census form- how would you answer? Some people refuse:

Why was the term 'Hispanic' generated in 1973 for government purposes?

Identify the biggest Hispanic groups in the USA: Identify the biggest Asian groups in the USA:

Is Hispanic regarded as an ethnicity or a race? Why?

How does the African American settlement pattern in Michigan demonstrate ethnic clustering?

African-Americans and Hispanics are more likely to live in: *cities*   *suburbs*   *rural areas*

Contrast Hispanic settlement in New York City versus the rest of New York state:

Regional ethnic clustering

Urban ethnic clustering

Within a country, where do ethnicities tend to cluster? _____

Identify the regional scale clustering of the following:

    HISPANICS   AFRICAN AMERICANS   ASIAN AMERICANS

Identify the urban scale clustering of the following:

HISPANICS	AFRICAN AMERICANS	ASIAN AMERICANS

Triangle trade

Emancipation Proclamation

Involuntary migration

Voluntary migration

Draw a big triangle in the space at right, and state what was traded on each leg of Triangle Trade:

What do St. Luis de Senegal, Goree Island, Fort James, Bruce Island, Sherbro, Elmina Castle, Cape Coast Castle, Annamabu, Whydah, Old Calabra, Bonny, Brass, Loango Bay, Malemba, Cabinda Mpina and Luanda all have in common?

_____

Historically, how was immigration to the USA different for Asians and Hispanics than for Africans?

_____

African-Americans have undergone four distinct migrations in US history. Summarize where, when and why:

1

2

3

4

How and why did African-American ghettos expand significantly after 1970?

Sharecropper

Ghetto

White Flight

Blockbusting

Graph 235: After black migration to Detroit and the race riots that happened during the 1960s, the following demographic changes occurred:

Whites went from _____ to _____, while blacks went from _____ then to _____.

Plessy v. Ferguson

Jim Crow

Brown v. Board of Education

Cultural segregation

Apartheid

Boer

Afrikaans

Homelands

Circle the following term(s) that tend to racially integrate society as opposed to segregate:

"Separate but Equal"   White Flight   Brown v. Board of Education

What is a Jim Crow law, where were they utilized, and for what purpose?

When the Detroit Institute of Arts opened in 1927, Detroit demographics were: 96% white, 4% black. European paintings were bought and donated to the museum, which the city called it its "crown jewel." Today, Detroit's demographics are 82% black, 7% white, 5% Hispanic, 5% Mixed and 1% Asian. A Museum of African American History was built in the 1960s, but the city is bankrupt and cannot fund both. Which should it fund? If you were a lawyer, how would you argue for them:

EUROPEAN-STYLE DIA   *AFRICAN AMERICAN HISTORY MUSEUM*

How did the apartheid system in South Africa work?

On the following timeline, write in the major event in South Africa's history:

1652_____1795_____1948_____1991_____1994
   \   \   \   \   \

Pg. 238   7 – ETHNICITY - Key Issue 3/4   Name_____

In the future, will our ethnicity will be 'Earthling?'

Nationality

American nationality

Quebecois

English

Welsh

Scots

Irish

UK

Six Nations

Nationalism

Flags, songs, symbols

Centripetal force

Centrifugal force

How is nationality different than ethnicity or race in common usage?

Nationality:

Ethnicity:

Race:

While Native Americans and Inuit peoples are distinct races in Canada from the majority, within the white group are varying ethnicities, such as the following:

1   2

In the UK, what are the characteristics of each principal *ethnicity*:

English: *Welsh:*

Scots: *Irish:*

What are the characteristics of the two primary *nationalities*:

British: *Irish:*

___

In 2014, Scotland voted to stay in the UK (narrowly). In a future referendum, how might the arrangement of *nationalities* in the British Isles change?

___

Golfer Tiger Woods' nationality is _____, but since he is tri-racial, with white, black and Asian genes, so how does he describe his ethnicity?

___

If racism is loyalty and favoritism to one's own biological race, while ethnocentrism is favoritism toward one's own ethnicity, what is nationalism?

___

Note some centripetal forces that pull nations of people together:

___

Note some centrifugal forces that push nations of people apart:

___

If you were fighting another nation in war, and wanted to destroy or undermine that existing nation, would you focus on encouraging centripetal forces or centrifugal forces among their population? Why?

___

Lebanese Civil War

Maronites

Sinhalese

Tamils

Moors

Map 240: At right, sketch the map of Lebanon and show the religious geography of the country:

The Druze have *gained*   *fallen* in population since the 1943 Lebanese constitution was passed.

How did that demographic change help lead to the civil war of 1975?

_____

What is the current status and future projection for stability in Lebanon?

_____

Map 241: Sketch the map of Sri Lanka at right, and indicate the religious and ethnic geography:

Label the ethnic group areas.
What languages doe they speak
and what religion is each?

1_____

2_____

3_____

What factors suppressed the usual violence between these ancient neighbors for the last 300 years, and why did it flare up again?

_____

_____

Pakistan _____

Bangladesh _____

Mahatma Gandhi _____

Kashmir _____

Punjab _____

Kurds _____

Kurdistan _____

The world's largest forced-migration of peoples occurred in the late-1940s in _____.

What tragically happened to some of the refugees as they migrated from one area to another?

_____

Many Muslims traveled _____ to Pakistan and _____ (the future Bangladesh), while many Hindus traveled _____ to India from Pakistan and _____ to India from Bangladesh.

Why is Kashmir a contentious issue right now? _____

Describe the Kurds of the Middle East:

| *Ethnicity* | *Language* | *Religion* | *Culture* |

In what countries to Kurds live today? | Why isn't there a Kurdistan?

After the deposing of Saddam Hussein, American leaders expected happiness from Iraqis, who were now free of a noted dictator. They didn't study the human geography. What did they get instead?

WELCOMED **OPPOSED** **OPPOSED**

Iran, the former Persian Empire, is an often-neglected topic of study but is a very important country. What are modern Iran's major ethnic identities:

Describe the ethnic diversity of:

AFGHANISTAN   **PAKISTAN**

Ethnic cleansing

Balkan peninsula

Yugoslavia

Dayton Accords

Balkanization

How is ethnic cleansing different than genocide? _____

_____

After WWII and the Allied victory, Polish territory was taken and awarded to the Soviet Union under pressure from Stalin, despite the fact he was on the Allied side and so was Poland. In compensation, the Allies gave Poland some German territory on the other side of the country. In 1946, entire cities and villages of Poles were told to pack up their things and move west from their homes that were given to the Soviets, to homes taken from Germans. The entire city of Wilno (Vilnius) migrated to the city of Szczecin (Stettin), while the whole city of Lwow (Lviv) moved to Wroclaw (Breslau). They were not the only ones who moved.

Is this an example of ethnic cleansing or genocide? _____

Map 246. How many Germans were ethnically cleansed from orange eastern territories? _____

During the communist era in Yugoslavia, which began after WWII, they used to say "Yugoslavia has..."

Five _____ which are _____

Four _____ which are _____

Three _____ which are _____

Two   _____ which are _____

One   _____ which is _____

How did it hold together- or rather, how was it held together?   After the end of communism, what happened to the ethnic situation in Yugoslavia?

_____

What agreements came out of the Dayton Accords in 1996? Which ethnicity got the 'best deal?'

_____

The most recent part of the region to split off was Kosovo from Serbia. What ethnic groups are at odds as to the fate of this territory, considered holy ground by some and home by others?

_____ and _____ - which side did the USA support? _____

What is the current status of Kosovo _____

Who is not happy about that? _____

Sudanese genocide	
Darfur	
Eritrean war	
Somali clans	
Rwandan genocide	
Congolese civil war	
Non-ethnic (imposed) boundary	

Pg. 252. For each of the following situations in Africa, summarize the ethnic conflict going on:

Sudan – South Sudan:

Sudan – Darfur:

Ethiopia vs. Eritrea:

Somalia:

Summarize the situation of the Hutu tribe of Central Africa and the Tutsis:

Hutu	*Tutsi*

When Rwanda and Burundi obtained independence from Europe, what happened there?

For each of the following situations in Africa, summarize the ethnic conflict going on:

Congo:

Map 255. Do any of Africa's political boundaries match the ethnic/tribal boundaries?

Pg. 261   8 - POLITICAL GEOGRAPHY – Key Issue 1/2   Name_____

You live in a state, unless you live on Sealand, the Moon, or the University of Antarctica. Then you live in a micronation, or something very like it.

State _____

Sovereignty _____

Microstates _____

Another name for state is _____, while another name for sovereignty is _____

United Nations _____

Security Council _____

The UN was established in _____ by _____.

Why did the UN grow so much in the following years?

1955   *1960s*   *1990s*

Before the UN was an attempt at an international organization called

_____

It existed during the years:

_____

List the 5 permanent members of the Security Council:

1   2   3

4   5   Is your country one of them? _____

So far in this decade, one state has been added to the UN. What is it? _____

Think back to last chapter- which other UN member(s) might not be happy about it becoming a fellow member?

_____

Might United Nations membership expand beyond the current level in the future?

Antarctica status _____

By what treaties have the Arctic and Antarctic been declared 'neutral' territory?

Do you think other countries should be able to claim Antarctica? Why or why not?

If climate change melts some of the ice off of Antarctica, exposing significant areas of land, how might this affect the territorial claims over it made before the treaties were signed- and what if there are resources found there?

How many sovereign states are there in the world? The book says ~200, but really it depends on who you ask. Each of the following, for example, can be considered one state or two. Make the case they are one state, and then two, as if you were a lawyer arguing both sides of the case:

ONE KOREA   **A NORTH AND A SOUTH KOREA**

ONE CHINA   **A TAIWAN AND A CHINA**

Is there or is there not a Sahrawi Republic? Make the case for yes and no:

YES THERE IS   **NO THERE IS NOT**

Is there an Islamic State of Iraq and Syria (ISIS)? This isn't in the book but make the case- does ISIS exist where ISIS forces are in control, such as the area around Raqqa in Syria, and northern "Iraq":

ISIS IS A STATE   **ISIS IS NOT A STATE**

Fertile Crescent _____

City-state _____

Empire _____

Medieval kingdom _____

Nation-state _____

Self-determination _____

Versailles Treaty _____

Principles developed in various eras of history related to state organization and function are, in summary:

ANCIENT STATES   *MEDIEVAL STATES*   *RISE OF NATION-STATES*

_____

Multiethnic state _____

Multinational state _____

Denmark and Slovenia _____

Socialist realism _____

Give an example of a multiethnic state   What is a good example of a multinational state?

_____   _____

In the example you gave, what are the nations contained in the multinational state?

_____

Why is Denmark a good example of a nation-state?   Is Slovenia also a good example? Why or why not?

_____   _____

Does the political principle of self-determination encourage or discourage nation-states? Why?

Three communist countries broke apart at the end of communism in the 1990s: Soviet Russia, Czechoslovakia and Yugoslavia. What kind of art did the communists encourage to foster a sense of class identity instead of national identity among the workers and peasants of their societies?

___

Why did the communists alter the clock in Olomouc, Czechoslovakia? Why bother?

___

The Soviet states broke into four regional collections plus Russia. The four collections are:

Collection	Countries
1	
2	
3	
4	

What is the majority population's percentage in the three Baltic States?

LITHUANIANS **ESTONIANS** **LATVIANS**

___

Remember last chapter when it said China was moving ethnic Han Chinese into Tibet on purpose to dilute Tibetan identity? What do you think the most prominent minority in the Baltic States is after decades of Soviet rule? _____.

Describe the situation in Moldova- why might this small state break apart further?

___

Discuss the religious and ethnic issues in the Central Asian 'Stan' countries:

___

In Russia itself, how many ethnicities are found there? _____

What nationalities actively want their own state? Why has Russia not to 'let them go?'

___

Caucasus states _____

Azerbaijan _____

Armenia _____

Georgia _____

Chechens _____

Dagestan _____

Ossetia _____

Nakhichevan _____

Nagorno-Karabakh _____

Discuss the religious and ethnic issues in the three Caucasus countries:

    AZERBAIJAN   *ARMENIA*   *GEORGIA*

Could new boundaries be based on the location of ethnicities in the Caucasus countries without ethnic cleansing? Why or why not?

Circle: The fall of communism   *strengthened*   *weakened*   ethnic identity in the region.

What evidence can you provide to support the one you circled?

How is a colony different than a state? _____

Three motivations for countries to collect colonies were, or are:

1   **2**   **3**

How is imperialism different that colonialism?

Map 274: Look at the green. Why did they used to say the sun never set on the British Empire?

Pg. 276   8 - POLITICAL GEOGRAPHY – Key Issue 3/4   Name_____

Alaska is the last frontier, and space is the final frontier. It knows no boundary

Boundary _____

Frontier _____

Physical boundary _____

Cultural boundary _____

Desert boundary _____

Mountain boundary _____

Water boundary _____

Law of the Sea _____

How is a frontier different than a boundary? _____

Some characteristics of frontiers are:

TYPE OF BOUNDARY	ADVANTAGE	EXAMPLE
DESERT		
MOUNTAIN		
WATER		

Draw the Law of the Sea graphic including the numbers:

CULTURAL BOUNDARY	EXAMPLE
1	
2	

Geometric boundary _____

Ethnic boundary _____

Green Line boundary

Describe the situation on Cyprus. Draw a map at right with the ethnic boundary:

_____

_____

_____

_____

SHAPE	GEOPOLITICAL ISSUE	EXAMPLE
1		
2		
3		
4		
5		
6		

Is it considered an advantage or disadvantage to be a landlocked state? Why?

_____

Most of the landlocked states are in _____, and the reason is:

_____

Landlocked state

National government

Democracy

Autocracy

Anocracy

Trend toward democracy

Arab Spring

Unitary state _____

Federal state _____

The type of 'regime' a state has is another way to say its type of _____

Brainstorm a strength and weakness for each type:

AUTOCRACY   **DEMOCRACY**

What reasons does the book give for the trend toward democracy?

How is a unitary different than a federal state? Circle the term 'whereas' in your answer:

Two conditions that encourage the formation of a unitary state are:

1

2

Examples of unitary states are:

Discuss the internal political organization of France:

Three conditions that encourage the formation of a federal state are:

1

2

3

Belgium is weird because it fits the profile of a unitary state but is a federal state. Why?

China is weird because it fits the profile of a federal state but is a unitary state. Why?

Classify what happened in each state during the Arab Spring:

OVERTHROW OF GOVERNMENT	CIVIL DISORDER/CHANGES	PROTESTS

Gerrymandering

Wasted vote

Excess vote

Stacked vote

Why do states bother redrawing their internal legislative boundaries periodically? What is at stake?

How does ethnicity influence this legislative redrawing?

(If you can, at this point look online. Search the name of your state and the term "congressional districts." A map should come up and you can see which is the most gerrymandered district in your state. Is it yours?)

Alliance

Cold War

NATO

Balance of power

Superpowers

Cuban Missile Crisis

Warsaw Pact

Hungary 1956

Czechoslovakia 1968

What is the idea behind the 'Balance of Power' concept?

_____

A not-so-funny joke is that WWI was fought with machine guns, WWII was fought with planes and bombs, WWIII will be fought with nukes, and WWIV will be fought with sticks and stones. What do you think the joke means?

_____

Could it happen? Nuclear annihilation? The Cuban Missile Crisis has been called the closest the world has ever come to it actually happening. Describe what went down:

_____

_____

_____

EU stands for _____. It was formed in _____

by _____.

The EU's stated purpose is:

Some states that want to join the EU are:

_____

Most countries in the EU have adopted this form of currency (money): _____

What may happen as a result of the Eurozone crisis? _____

REGIONAL ORGANIZATION	MEMBERS	PURPOSE
OSCE		
OAS		
AU		
COMMONWEALTH		

_____

The typical definitions of terrorism reflect the following three characteristics:

1   2   3

Terrorism _____

Committee of Public Safety _____

Assassination _____

Sept. 11th attacks _____

Osama bin Laden _____

Al-Qaeda _____

Fatwa _____

"Terrorism" is not a new activity. Early modern terrorism was used during the French Revolution by the Jacobins, a group of political radicals who despised the monarchy, and executed the king, queen and thousands of other people, often without trial or on the trumped up charge of being "an enemy of the revolution."

Who was the leader of this guillotine-happy radical party? _____

Is assassination of famous people considered terrorism? _____

What makes terrorism different than other kinds of political violence like declaring wars?

_____

Name some places Americans were targeted by terrorist groups in the 20th century:

1	2
3	4
5	6

What role did Afghanistan play in Sept. 11? _____

Note the major incidents claimed to have been perpetrated by the Al-Qaeda group:

1	2
3	4
5	6
7	8
9	10

The news doesn't focus on terrorism in Indonesia- list the significant incidents there:

1   2

3   4

5   6   7

Taliban

Mujahedeen

Bin-Laden compound

Where was bin-Laden eventually found? _____. Were they close? _____

How have the following states been thought to support terrorism in the past or present:

LIBYA   *IRAQ*   *IRAN*   *PAKISTAN*   *OTHERS?*

Post-9/11 attacks

Saddam Hussein

WMDs

"Regime change"

Shah Mohammad Reza Pahlavi

Iran-Iraq War

Nuclear proliferation

Mummar el-Qaddafi

Heartland Theory / Halford Mackinder*

Rimland Theory / Nicholas Spykman*

Pg. 298.   9 – DEVELOPMENT – Key Issues 1/2   Name of Person_____

Do not go home today and cut down the trees in your yard, telling your mom, when she demands to know what you are doing, "development."

Development _____

HDI _____

Is the street your house is on paved? _____. If yes, it is a level up in development from where streets are unpaved. Unpaved roads cause more tire blowouts, wear on cars, and contain, therefore, hidden costs that would be lessened if the roads were paved (which also costs money). Draw a line representing *Trans-African Highway 8*, placing dashes in places the road is unpaved:

Lagos	Yaounde	Bangui	Kisangani	Kampala	Nairobi	Mombasa
Nigeria	Cameroon	C.A.R.	Congo	Uganda	Kenya	Kenya

Start_____   _____Finish

Who paid for this highway across Africa? _____

GNI _____

PPP _____

GDP _____

Primary sector _____

Secondary sector _____

Tertiary sector _____

Quaternary sector* _____

Quinary sector* _____

Productivity _____

Value added _____

Inequality-adjusted HDI _____

When calculating a state's ranking on the HDI, the UN considers these three things:

1   2   3

The four categories your country might wind up in are:

1   2   3   4

Summarize the general place on the HDI scale the following regions inhabit:

North America _____ **Europe** _____

Latin America _____ **East Asia** _____

Central Asia _____ **Southeast Asia** _____

Middle East _____ **South Asia** _____

Sub-Saharan Africa _____ **Your Country** _____

Do all countries have the same cost of living? _____

Would you rather live in New York making 100,000/year or in Tampa, FL making 70,000/year, but only having half the expenses for housing, food, car, and all the rest being of the same quality?

"Per capita GDP measures average (mean) wealth, not its distribution." What does this mean in human terms?

SECTOR OF ECONOMY	TYPES OF JOBS	SPECIFIC EXAMPLES
PRIMARY		
SECONDARY		
TERTIARY		

Are more people- as a percentage- primary sector workers in MDCs or LDCs _____
(MDC = developed country, LDC = developing country)

Give a specific example of a value added phenomenon:

If a country's IHDI is low, the country probably has a lot of _____

Which country has a more equalized society, the USA or Canada _____

Map 303. Name a country with a high IHDI,
where most people have a similar standard of living:
(usually this is an indicator of a developed economy   _____
where most people are middle class)

Name a country with a low IHDI, usually an indicator of a lot of poor and a few rich people _____

Consumer goods

Life expectancy

Three consumer goods are reliable measures of a state's level of development. What are they?

1   2   3

If you do have good access to consumer goods, and you live in a developing country, where in that country do you probably live, and why:

_____

While doctor-patient ratios in the developed world are _____,

while in the developing world they are _____.

What is the role of diet (as in what people eat) on people's health in MDCs vs. LDCs?

Item	Developed	Developing
Life expectancy		
Infant mortality rate		
Number of young people		

The world region with the highest life expectancy is _____, the lowest is _____

Years of schooling

Expected YOS

Pupil/teacher ratio

Literacy rate

A greater percentage of kids go to school   a. near the equator   b. at 50 degrees N. Latitude

Circle: School classes tend to have more students in   a. *developed*   b. *developing*   countries.

While the literacy rate in Australia is _____%___, in Africa it is _____%___.

Changing scale to 'sub-national' means making it: a. larger   b. smaller   c. the same

On a local scale, what is something China, Mexico and Brazil all have in common?

_____

List the states of the following large countries where people have the highest incomes:

    BRAZIL (2)   *CHINA (7)*   *MEXICO (3)*

_____

Pg. 309. A country with a small population and a life expectancy over .9 is _____

A country with a small population and a life expectancy under .5 is _____

A country with a large population and a life expectancy under .6 is _____

GII _____

Empowerment _____

Female labor force participation rate _____

Maternal mortality ratio _____

GDI considers three specific areas, they are

1   2   3

The countries with the highest GDIs are: The countries with the lowest GDIs are:

_____

Where do women tend to be in lawmaking positions in government? _____

What percentage of legislators are women? _____ How about in the USA _____

Adolsecent fertility rate measures number of girls that have kids between _____ and _____
Rate 3 countries in each of the following adolescent fertility rate categories:

    HIGH   **MEDIUM**   **LOW**
60+/1,000 girls   20-59/1,000 girls   0-19/1,000 girls

Pg. 314. 9 – DEVELOPMENT – Key Issues 3/4 Name of Person_____
"Time to find some energon cubes" -Megatron

Supply

Demand

Coal

Petroleum

Natural gas

Fossil fuel

Where do each of the following sources of energy come from?

COAL	PETROLEUM	NATURAL GAS

"Quad"

BTU

Renewable energy

Nonrenewable energy

Fossil fuels are: *renewable*   *nonrenewable*   sources of energy.

The Mesozoic (dinosaur era) gave way to the Cenozoic (mammal era) 65,000,000 years ago. On which side of the Gulf of Mexico, east or west, are the most proven reserves? _____

Proven reserves

Potential reserve

Fracking

Where are the following sources of energy located across the world?

COAL	PETROLEUM	NATURAL GAS

Think science and time… lots of time: How is it that fossil fuels are now found at the mid-latitudes when they form in tropical jungles? Circle the word 'tectonic' in your answer!

_____

What is OPEC and which countries are in it? _____

_____

Why did American cars all of a sudden become smaller and more gas efficient around 1980?

_____

Sketch the graph on pg. 320 on the history of oil prices since 1970:

D b
O p a
L e r
L r r
A e
R l
S l

1970   1980   1990   2000   2010   now

What does "adjusted for inflation" mean on the red line as opposed to the absolute price (blue line?):

_____

Nuclear energy _____

Fission _____

Radioactive waste _____

Uranium _____

Breeder reactor _____

Hydroelectric _____

Biomass fuel _____

Wind power _____

Geothermal _____

Fusion _____

Passive solar energy

Space solar power (SSP)*

There are ups and downs for every type of alternative energy to fossil fuels. You get to identify them:

	POSITIVES	NEGATIVES
NUCLEAR		
HYDROELECTRIC		
BIOMASS		
WIND		
GEOTHERMAL		
FUSION		
PASSIVE SOLAR		
ACTIVE SOLAR		

Self-sufficiency

International trade

India's strategy

Walt Rostow

Rostow Model

1

2

3

4	
5	
Asian Dragons	
Arab Gulf States	
WTO	
WTO protests	

Complete the chart by taking notes on the two models of development:

	SELF SUFFICIENTY MODEL	**INTERNATIONAL TRADE APPROACH (Rostow)**
E L E M E N T S		

What was India's experience with the self-sufficiency model like?

Summarize the Four Asian Dragons' experience with development:	Summarize the Arab Gulf States' situation with development:
SELF-SUFFICIENCY MODEL CHALLENGES	**INTERNATIONAL TRADE CHALLENGES**

Most geographers argue the _____ model has shown the most success. Why is this?

1

2

3

4

5

6

7

FDI

World Bank

IMF

What is the position of the WTO on the following items?

Self-sufficiency vs. International trade:

Import quotas:

Export tariffs:

Flow of money / FDI:

What criticisms have conservatives had for the WTO?   How about liberal criticism?

Review: how is a transnational corporation different from a local or national one?

Structural Adjustment Program

Stimulus strategy

Austerity strategy

Housing bubble

The two ways LDCs usually get money to finance development are:

1   2

The two main sources for loans for LDCs are: 1   2
Where do you think *they* get the money to loan?

Theory and practice are not always the same. Theory is what is supposed to happen, practice is what actually happens. In practice, what has happened over half the time in Africa when loans for development programs like infrastructure have been provided:

1

2

3

Map 333. What three regions do NOT get any money from the World Bank?

1   2   3

                              does yours? _____

Why are structural adjustment programs controversial even though they are trying to clean up the corruption and make development happen by requiring the country's leaders to make the six changes on 334?

	Requirements	**Controversy**
1		
2		
3		
4		
5		
6		

Why did many Americans become angry when large government 'bailouts' funded by U.S. taxpayers and businesses, were given to large banks that made irresponsible loans?

Contrast: STIMULUS STRATEGY   AUSTERITY STRATEGY

How is the 2008 housing bubble bursting similar to the Dutch tulip bulb bubble bursting in 1637- what happened in both cases to prices for the items in question?

Fair trade

Fair trade coffee

Microfinance

Millennium development goals

1

2

3

4

6

7

8

Uneven development

Core

Periphery

Immanuel Wallerstein*

World System Theory*

* Look it up online and define. It is always on the test but for some reason it is not in the book.

Pg. 347   10 – AGRICULTURE – Key Issues 1/2   Name_____

Yum! (Until you know where it comes from)

Agriculture _____

Cultivation _____

Hunter-gatherers _____

Hunter-gatherer society is characterized by the following:

_____

Pic 347: About how many hunter-gatherers like this man are there left worldwide? _____.

Where are they located? _____

Agricultural revolution _____

Crop hearth _____

Animal diffusion _____

Identify crops domesticated in each region based on how much you'd like to consume it:

SW Asia	*East Asia*	*Africa*	*Americas*
1	1	1	1
2	2	2	2
3	3	3	3
4	4	4	4

The _____ was domesticated in Central Asia by early Europeans, while these animals were domesticated in SW Asia:

1   2   3   4

FYI: This person produced the most widely used agricultural map of the world: *Derwent Whittlesey.*

Subsistence agriculture _____

Commercial agriculture _____

Farming and GPS _____

Farm size _____

Contrast the items below between their applications in LDC and MDC farming

	% farmers	Machine use	Farm size
Developing Countries			
Developed Countries			

Dietary energy consumption

Kcal

Cereal

Wheat

Rice

Maize

Other crops

What is the world's most 'typical' human? Where do they live and what do they do?

If you live in an English speaking country, what is likely your leading source of protein? _____

If you add Ethiopia's number of undernourished people to the rest of Africa, does it equal India? _

Undernourishment

Graph 355 (top): Draw the wheel of undernourishment, and place a star next to your region's 'slice' below:

Graph 355 (bot.): Of the seven regions, list them from most people undernourished to least:

1   2

3   4

5   6

7   **Circle your region**

Pg. 356   10 – AGRICULTURE – Key Issues 3/4   Name_____
Time to enter the Meatrix

Pastoral nomadism _____

Shifting agriculture _____

Intensive subsistence- rice _____

Intensive subsistence- other _____

Plantation _____

Mixed crop and livestock _____

Dairying _____

Grain _____

Ranching _____

Mediterranean _____

Commercial gardening _____

The kinds of agricultural activity that predominate in developed differs from in developing countries. List the types:

	DEVEOPING	**DEVEOPED**
1		
2		
3		
4		
5		
6		

Pastoral nomadism _____

Transhumance _____

Pasture _____

How does pastoral nomadism differ from the hunter-gatherer lifestyle?

Where are most pastoral nomads located? _____

Describe the sense of territoriality amongst pastoral nomads and how transhumance factors in:	Why don't modern governments quite know what to do with pastoral nomads?

*For a look at pastoral nomadism, Youtube the 1925 movie *Grass*. It was filmed live in Central Asia before global civilization arrived there.

The two major characteristics of shifting cultivation are

1   2

The two major hallmarks of the technique of shifting cultivation are

1   2

The crops usually farmed using shifting cultivation are _____

Describe land ownership in villages where shifting cultivation is practiced:

_____

_____ % of humans practice shifting cultivation, utilizing about _____ % of the world's land.
*They gave you the stats- figure it out

Shifting cultivation: **PROs**   **CONs**

Slash and burn _____

Swidden _____

Kayapo _____

Intensive subsistence _____

Sawah/Paddy _____

Chaff _____

Threshing _____

Winnowing _____

Hull _____

Double cropping

Where is intensive subsistence- wet rice practiced and why is it practiced there?

_____

The stages of wet rice growing are:

	Stage	**Characteristics**
1		
2		
3		
4		

Where is it possible to practice 'double-cropping' and where is it not?

Yes:	No:

There are four pics on page 362-363. What stage do they most go with?

1 Philippines: 2 Japan:

3 Malaysia: 4 Thailand:

What other crops are farmed by people practicing intensive subsistence agriculture?

_____

In China, agriculture has changed a lot since the communist revolution of 1949. Contrast then and now:

COMMUNE SYSTEM	**NEW SYSTEM**

When:

Characteristics:

Plantation

What kind of crops are favored by plantation farmers? _____

What climates are favorable for plantation farming? _____

Plantation farms are owned by _____ and worked by _____

Pg. 365 where are the people in the picture being transported? _____

Agribusiness

Crop rotation _____

Truck farming _____

Where is mixed crop and livestock farming practiced? _____

Why does the book say is ironic about the amount of land devoted to crops vs. to animals and the income each produces?

_____

Why does this kind of agriculture allow farmers to more evenly distribute their workload?

_____

The US Corn Belt is located _____, _____ is becoming a popular crop.

Name some ways the versatile crop *corn* is used besides eating as corn-on-the-cop:

_____

Think of the concept of crop rotation. What is the role of each of the following:

    Cereal grain   *fallow*   *rest crop*

_____

Where in the USA is commercial gardening and fruit farming practiced? _____
What three conditions make it so?

1   *2*   *3*

The target market for truck farmers is _____.

They keep costs down by employing these three strategies:

1   *2*   *3*

Dairy farming _____

Grain farming _____

Combine _____

Winter wheat _____

Spring wheat _____

Palouse region

Mediterranean horticulture

_____ is the world's largest producer of dairy products.

Some places specialize in cheese, butter and cream but not regular milk.

Where are these places	Why are they not focusing on milk?

List some challenges for a dairy farmer that other farmers don't have to worry about as much:

Grain Farming- name the reasons wheat is such an important crop:

What makes the Mediterranean climate special? _____

What kind of crops are harvested in this climate? _____

Of these, two are big cash crops. They are _____ and _____.

Parts of California have a Mediterranean climate. What is the role of these regions (Napa Valley) on Mediterranean agriculture?

If you ran a combine company, how would you use your understanding of the spring and winter wheat belts to maximize your productivity (and hence your profits!)?	What's the difference between fixed location ranching and open range cattle drives? Which was first?

Ranching

Commercial ranching

Summarize ranching in…

Europe *South America* *Australia*

List some ways subsistence farmers tend to go about their production:

	Type	Meaning
1		
2		
3		
4		
5		
6		
7		

Boserup's new methods

Boserup's fallow method

Sahel famine issue

What has happened to per capita food per person in Africa between 1960, when the population was 300 million, and today, when the population is over 1 billion?

Drug crop

Drug crops are often illegal, but highly profitable in a way peanuts and beans might not be. What is the story behind each of the following:

Coca leaf   **Marijuana**   **Opium/Heroin**

Why are food prices projected to go up instead of down or stay the same?

_____

_____

_____

Draw the food price graph on pg. 377, label everything at right:

The USA has had (circle):   **overproduction**   **underproduction**   of many crops.

The US government has tried three strategies to help farmers. Note those strategies

STRATEGY	EXPLANATION AS TO WHY
1	
2	
3	

Farm subsidies in the USA differ from those in Europe. How?

Overproduction

Von Thunen model

Johann Heinrich von Thunen

Draw the Von Tunen model at right, and label the rings:

First ring:

Second ring:

Third ring:

Fourth ring:

Assumptions made by the Von Thunen model:

Increasing exports

Expanding agricultural land

Desertification

Prime agricultural land

List the four strategies to increase agricultural output to feed hungry people:

1   3

2   4

Expanding fishing

Aquaculture

Do you check if your fish is from an aquaculture fish farm or caught in the wild?   Y   N

Do you check if your fish farm produced fish have been treated with antibiotics?   Y   N

Is seafood consumption at an all time high right now? _____

Is more seafood consumed in the developed world than in the developing? _____

What is happening to ¾ of the world's species of fish due to human population growth?

Green revolution

GM food

Sustainable agriculture

Ridge tillage

Monsanto

'Roundup ready'

Esther Boserup

The Green Revolution favored two practices new to farming. What were they?

What is the controversy surround GM crops? If you were a lawyer, argue for an against their being legal to farm and available in stores:

| **LEGAL GM** | **BAN GM** |

Sustainable agriculture has three main bases. Summarize each as you read:

| **LAND MANAGEMENT** | **LIMITED CHEMICALS** | **CROP + LIVESTOCK** |

Pg. 395 11 – INDUSTRY – Key Issues 1/2 NAME_____

Yuck. Except when I need a job. Or almost any modern convenience.

Industrial revolution _____

Iron _____

Coal _____

Transportation _____

Textiles _____

Chemicals _____

Food processing _____

In which country did the Industrial Revolution begin?   Where did it spread?

_____   _____

Talk about some ways the Industrial Revolution changed the world:

_____

The steam engine was invented by _____ (in science what do you measure power in?)

The first industries impacted by the Industrial Revolution were:

	INDUSTRY	**HOW IT WAS IMPACTED**
1		
2		
3		
4		
5		
6		

UK _____

Rhine-Ruhr _____

Mid-Rhine _____

Po Basin

Northeastern Spain

Moscow environs

St. Petersburg

Urals

Volga basin

Kuznetsk

Donetsk

Silesia

New England

Middle Atlantic

Mohawk Valley

Pittsburgh-Lake Erie

Western Great Lakes

Southern California

Southeastern Ontario

Japan

China

Korea

Proximity to inputs

Proximity to markets

Bulk-reducing industry

Nonmetallic minerals

Metallic minerals

Ferrous alloy

Ferrous _____

Uses of Chromium _____

Uses of Manganese _____

...Molybdenum _____

Nickel _____

Tin _____

Titanium _____

Tungsten _____

Nonferrous metal _____

Aluminum _____

Copper _____

Lead _____

Lithium _____

Magnesium _____

Zinc _____

Precious metals _____

Rare earth metals _____

What are two types of situation factors:

1   2

Why do some industries locate near inputs and some not?

DO: **DON'T:**

_____

Yum! Minerals! Earth has _____ natural elements. 99 percent is made of:

There are about _____ different minerals, either _____ or _____.

Most (90%) of nonmetallic minerals are _____

What nonmetallic minerals are in fertilizer? _____

P is for: *K is for:*

Ca is for: *S is for:*

Would you like an internship in an Indonesian sulfur mine? _____

What are nonmetallic gemstones used for? _____
*You know this... think about it

What are ferrous alloys used for? _____

Name 8 of them and their major characteristic:

	ITEM	CHARACTERISTIC	LOCATION
1			
2			
3			
4			
5			
6			
7			
8			

What are nonferrous metals used for? _____

Name 8 of them and their major characteristic:

	ITEM	CHARACTERISTIC	LOCATION
1			
2			
3			
4			
5			
6			
7			
8			

Bulk-gaining industry _____

Beverage example _____

YKK zipper example _____

Perishable products _____

Why are the following bulk-gaining industries?

FABRICATED METALS	BEVERAGE PRODUCTION

What is different about single-market manufacturers? _____

Name some examples of 'perishable products' _____

Where must they be located? _____

Trucks _____

Trains _____

Ships _____

Air _____

Bulk-of-break-point _____

Gangue _____

Concentration _____

Smelting _____

Refining _____

Steel _____

TYPE OF TRANSPORT	ADVANTAGE	DISADVANTAGE
TRUCK		
TRAIN		
SHIP		
AIRPLANE		

The most expensive kind is _____, the cheapest is _____

What happens to shipping costs at break-of-bulk points? _____

Name some examples of BoB points: _____

Produce a flowchart showing how copper is a bulk-reducing industry:
*It better be good

_____

What role does energy play in the decisions about where a copper mill will be located?

_____

Why *was* Pittsburgh, PA such a good place for steel mills (so good in fact that the city's football team was named after the workers at steel mills!)

_____

Why did the area around Lake Erie and Southern Lake Michigan take primacy later on?

_____

How come the east and west coasts (Trenton, NJ and Los Angeles) took primacy after that?

_____

Characterize steel production today- how are the mills different, and are they closer or further to their intended markets than before- and why?

_____

Traditionally, American cars had been made in the Motor City (aka _____) called that to the point where its basketball team was named after the parts inside the cylinders of a car's engine that move up and down rapidly to make the car go.

Name two European countries cars are NOT made in _____ _____

Name two countries in South America that cars ARE made in _____ _____

Name two countries in Africa that cars ARE made in _____ _____

Name two Middle Eastern countries that cars ARE made in _____ _____

In Europe, what country makes the MOST cars? _____

Summarize where cars are made in the following regions:

NORTH AMERICA	EUROPE	EAST ASIA

The three factors of production are _____, _____ and _____

Pg. 409. Honda's main concerns in locating a plant (its *critical situation factor*), were:

Its critical *site* factors were _____

Where did Honda finally build its new plant? _____. What and where is

Auto Alley? _____

Labor-intensive industry _____

Labor _____

Capital _____

Land _____

Apparel _____

The five major countries for cotton yard production are: 1

2   3   4   5

The six major countries for cotton weaving are: 1   2

3   4   5   6

Check the labels of something you are wearing made of cotton. Did it come from one of these places? _____

Pg. 412   11 – INDUSTRY – Key Issues 3/4   NAME_____

Air pollution is caused by the incineration of student work after it is graded, handed back, and thrown out

Air pollution _____

Global warming _____

Greenhouse effect _____

Ozone _____

CFCs _____

When does air pollution occur? _____

Our atmosphere consists of these elements: _____

The three human activities that generate the most air pollution are _____

Describe the greenhouse effect: _____

Venus is farther from the sun than Mercury. Why is it hotter? _____

Could global cooling ever be a problem do you think? When was it last a problem? (Look up Little Ice Age):

_____

Acid deposition _____

Acid precipitation _____

Carbon monoxide _____

Hydrocarbons _____

Smog _____

Particulates _____

Landfill _____

Hazardous waste _____

The 3 basic components of air pollution are: 2

1   3

_____ is the worst air pollution city in America, but most of the top 10 are in

_____ and _____.

NOTE SOME EXAMPLES OF TOXIC WASTE ISSUES?

_____

Point-source pollution _____

Nonpoint-source pollution _____

Aral sea _____

BOD _____

Summarize the point sources of water pollution:

      WATER-USING MANUFACTURERS   **MUNICIPAL SEWAGE**

_____

Nonpoint sources have contributed to the shocking shrinkage of the:

           _____ Sea in _____

What happened to his sea?   What is the forecast for this sea?

_____   _____

How does BOD affect a fish's bod-y? _____

TVA _____

Right-to-work law _____

Central Europe _____

Pg. 418. Location factors are changing. What factor is especially changing:

_____

Since the 1950s, industry has been shifting in the United States- and then out. But as far as the shifts within the USA go, what have been the essential trends? Describe it as if Henry Ford woke up from stasis and asked what had been going on for the last 60 years:

_____

Tell Ford about 'right to work' laws. What are they? And how have they contributed to the shift in where industries locate?

_____

_____

In Europe, a lot of manufacturing has shifted to the _____ in the last two decades.

Outsourcing
_____

New International Division of Labor
_____

Vertical integration
_____

NAFTA
_____

Maquiladoras
_____

BRICS
_____

Are you likely to make more of a wage in a convergence region or in a competitiveness region? ___

Out of land, labor and capital, which factor of production is most relevant concerning *outsourcing?*

_____

The more people willing to sell their labor for cheap, the more attractive your country is for outsourcing from expensive labor markets.   ***true***   ***false***

When companies vertically integrate, it contributes to outsourcing   ***true***   ***canard***

What is NAFTA? _____

What are some fears about NAFTA? _____

_____

Who is usually employed in a maquiladora _____

What is produced there _____

How many are there and where did they open_____

Why that location? _____

How has NAFTA affected Mexico and the United States _____

_____

Add up how much it costs Apple to make an iPod: Apple's U.S. profit is:

Why are so many electronics companies leaving Mexico for China? _____

A competitor to NAFTA is BRIC, now BRICS. What countries are in BRICS?

_____

What is the essential concept behind BRICS? Consider factors like land area, population and resources:

_____

_____

_____

With all that land, people and resources, what problems does BRICS face?

_____

_____

Fordist production _____

Post-Fordist production _____

Teams _____

Problem-solving _____

Leveling _____

Productivity _____

Just-in-time delivery _____

Contrast production styles:

FORDIST	**POST-FORDIST**

Give an example of a 'just-in-time' delivery:

_____

How is 'just-in-time' different than regular delivery services?

_____

How is 'just-in-time' different than regular delivery services?

_____

Labor unrest _____

Traffic _____

Natural hazards _____

American car _____

Steam Engine / James Watt* _____

Least-Cost Theory / Alfred Weber* _____

NAME AS MANY AS YOU CAN…

AMERICAN CAR COMPANIES	**FOREIGN COMPANIES**

Summarize the piece on what an American car actually is nowadays:

Pg. 431   12 – SERVICES – Key Issues 1/2   NAME_____
"Hey, hey, can we get some service over here? We've been waitin' 11 chapters already!"

Service _____

Consumer services come in four types- identify and provide an example

	Type of Consumer service	**An example:**
1		
2		
3		
4		

	Type of Business service	**An example:**
1		
2		
3		

How many levels of government are there if one worked in public service government? _____

What is the trend between 1972 and 2010 in the USA as far as service jobs go?

_____

The 2008 recession was in large part caused by issues related to the service sector. What five bullet points has Rubenstein identified as symptomatic of this recession?

1
2
3
4
5

Real estate speculation

Subprime mortgage

Key Issue 2. What is at the core of a market area? _____

Central place theory _____

Daily urban systems _____

Market area _____

Hinterland _____

Walter Christaller _____

Range _____

Threshold _____

Locate your daily urban system if you live in the USA. Hypothesize, what is the central place of your system?

_____

How far away is that central place from your house? _____ How often do you go there? _____

What about circles and squares make them inferior to hexagons as a way to graph central places?

Circles _____

Squares _____

Businesses with a long range include: Business with a short range include:

If the threshold is the minimum number of _____ necessary to sustain a service, how come all people are not counted equally in the equation?

_____

Contrast the differences between hamlets, villages, towns and cities:

Rank-size rule _____

Primate city rule _____

Summarize the situation in the following countries regarding the phenomenon listed:

	Rank-size rule	**Primate cities**
USA		
Mexico		

After geographers finish their market area analysis, where is the best location for a service once range and threshold have been accounted for?

Explain what the Gravity Model says about where to put a service:

Why do you think there are more Walmart stores around Dayton, OH than in the city itself?

Note the average occurrence of periodic markets in the following regions:

MUSLIM COUNTRIES	**CHINA**	**KOREA**	**AFRICA**

When:

Why:

Market area analysis

Gravity model

Periodic market

Locate your area of the country on the maps on pg. 441.

My area saw: STRONG GROWTH   WEAK GROWTH   SEVERE DECLINE   N/A

Where were the strong metro areas during the recession?

Where were the weak metro areas during the recession? Perhaps people didn't vacation as much?

Pg. 442   12 – SERVICES – Key Issues 3/4   NAME_____
Got talent?

Global cities

What makes global cities attractive to businesses? Make a list:

Do you live nearest to an alpha, beta or gamma city? Which one? _____

When was the last time you ever been to an alpha city?

W	Name the two A++ Global Cities	What do they share	Name the A+ GCs
O			
R			
L			
D			

Offshore centers provide the following:

1   2

Name some places that companies put money they don't want taxed:

Is a company more likely to move its headquarters or back offices to a developing country?_____

Why? _____

What is the economic base of a community?

What is the economic base of *your* community?

What are 7 different specializations that cities often have?

1	2	3	4
5	6	7	my city is a:

Offshore financial services

Taxes factor

Privacy factor

Cayman Islands

Business-process outsourcing

Call center

Low wage factor

English factor

Basic industries

Nonbasic industries

Economic base

Coolness Index

Name six factors Richard Florida used to determine distribution of talent in cities:

Name four cities that are tops in talent:
|
|
|
|
|

Is a city close to you a high talent city or a 'cool' city? _____. Where is the nearest one? ___

Clustered rural settlement

Dispersed rural settlement

Hamlet/village

Circular rural settlement

Kraal

Gewandorf _____

Linear-rural settlement _____

Long-lot farms _____

Clustered settlements _____

Common _____

Land grant _____

Frontier _____

Draw the shape of a clustered rural settlement: Draw a circular rural settlement:

Draw a linear rural settlement: Draw a dispersed rural settlement:

Colonial New England built _____ settlements for these three reasons:

1   2   3

What was the usual type of settlement in rural America during the colonial era- and why?

_____

In Britain, what was the role of the Enclosure Movement on the way rural people settled?

Note the progress in each type of service in early rural settlements:

| Consumer Services | Public Services | Business Services |

Enclosure movement

Urbanization

Mesopotamia/Ur

Greece/Athens

City-states

Imperial Rome

Feudal lords

Carcassonne

Largest cities: 100-500

Largest cities: 600-1800

Largest cities: 1900-2000 (today)

Note the progress in each phase of urban settlement:

| Ancient Cities | Medieval Cities |

Explain the two dimensions of urbanization:

1   2

Urbanization's two dimensions

Pg. 461   13 – URBAN PATTERNS – Key Issues 1/2   NAME_____

"Mom, thanks to your generation's outsourcing and urban blight, my generation has a lot of places to host raves and rap battles."

What does CBD stand for? _____. A.k.a.: "downtown".

CBD business services _____

CBD consumer services _____

CBD exclusions _____

Empty nesters _____

Why do high-end business services cluster in CBDs?	Do high threshold retailers locate in the CBD? What happened recently to them?

Why do high range retailers pick CBDs to locate in?	What kinds of retailers DO locate downtown?

Name an activity excluded from CBDs:

  1   why:

  2   why:

Do you ever go to a CBD? What do you do there?	Discuss how land prices in the CBD compare with land prices elsewhere:

Food desert _____

Underground CBD _____

Skyscrapers _____

Zoning ordinances _____

Two neat things about CBDs are underground 'cities' and skyscrapers. Note the characteristics:

UNDERGROUND CITY   **SKYCRAPERS**

What is Washington DC's rule about skyscrapers? _____

How people are distributed in an urban area is coming up on the next page in Key Issue 2. Are you excited? You should be. You are a person. And as such, you are about to get distributed. Where? Only Key Issue 2 knows that answer.

Concentric zone model _____

E.W. Burgess _____

1 _____

2 _____

3 _____

4 _____

5 _____

Sector model _____

Homer Hoyt _____

1 _____

2 _____

3 _____

4 _____

5 _____

Multiple nuclei model _____

Harris and Ullman _____

1 _____

2 _____

3 _____

4 _____

5 _____

6 _____

7 _____

8 _____

9 _____

        DRAW MODEL   **NAME CHARACTERISTICS AND FEATURES**

C
O
N
C
E
N
T
R
I
C

        DRAW MODEL   **NAME CHARACTERISTICS AND FEATURES**

S
E
C
T
O
R

M N
U U
L C
T L
I E
P I
L
E

Census tracts

Social area analysis

PRIZM cluster

The Census Bureau divides America's neighborhoods up into	What kind of census data is used in social area analyses?

Provide an example of segmentation:	Provide examples of PRIZM:

CBDs in Europe

Sectors in Europe

Concentric zones in Europe

How are European CBDs *different* than North American CBDs?

Draw an American CBD:
   Include skyscrapers

Draw a European CBD:
   Include churches and buildings like in fig. 13-16

Usually American city centers are ringed by lower income neighborhoods. Is that true for European cities?   Y   N

What was all the fuss about when the office tower Tour Montparnasse opened in Paris?

___

A spine is usually a large thoroughfare (a big road) stretching out from the CBD into the outskirts of the city, and along which upper class people live and hang out.

   a. true   b. false   c. this is way too small for me to see   d. a and c   e. a, c and d

Name an advantage to living along the southwestern spine of Paris:

Name an advantage to living in the inner ring:

___

Europe's poorer residents usually live in suburbs away from the city centers. List three characteristics about them:

1   2   3

Sectors in LDCs ___

Concentric zones in LDCs ___

Squatter settlements ___

Local names: ___

Precolonial city ___

Colonial city ___

Postcolonial city ___

Lake Texcoco ___

Do cities in developing countries resemble North American or European cities more? Why is that?

_____ Because...

___

Why do squatter settlements (shantytowns) tend to appear in a large ring around developing cities?

___

What kind of amenities and services does one often find in squatter settlements?

___

Describe the three stages in the development of a family building in a squatter settlement:

1

2

3

Draw the Latin American city model on pg. 472:

Most of the developing countries were former colonies of Europe sometime between 1492 and 1980. Consequently, there are native, European and postcolonial sectors of most older LDC cities. Contrast their various elements:

OLD QUARTERS (PRECOLONIAL CITY)	EUROPEAN DISTRICT (COLONIAL ADDITION)

What's the story behind the elite spine in Mexico City?

Pg. 476　　　13 – URBAN PATTERNS – Key Issues 3/4　　　NAME_____

College boy: "Hey so where are you from?"
College girl: Specify: MSA, uSA, CBSA, CSA, PCSA, 'urban area,' metropolitan typonym or functional region?
"Uh, what?"
Just messing with you. Some of those aren't even mutually exclusive.
"Uh, what?"
You didn't have human geography in high school, did you?

Peripheral model _____

Edge city _____

City _____

Urban area _____

Metropolitan area _____

MSA _____

uSA _____

CBSA _____

CSA _____

PCSA _____

Draw and label the elements of an urban area according to the Peripheral Model:

What number would the
Edge City in the model
On pg. 476 be?

_____

(hint: edge cities
contain office space)

How is an urban area different than a city?　　　A city and its suburbs all in a functioning region is called a

_____　　　_____

Megalopolis _____

Council of government _____

How might you know you were in a megalopolis?

The NE USA megalopolis runs from the nodes of Boston to _____.

It contains _____ percent of the whole US population on _____ percent of its land.

Over what kind of issue is a council of government most likely to meet?	How is a federation different than a council of government?

Annexation

Density gradient

Suburban sprawl

Greenbelts

Smart growth

In the past, peripheral areas of cities *wanted* to be annexed; now they do not. Why?

Can a suburb be a central city?	Y	N
Are suburbs included in MSAs?	Y	N
What three things does an MSA include?	1	
2	3	

Note two ways the density gradient has changed in recent years?

1   2

Why do conservationists usually argue sprawl is bad?

What is the rationale behind leaving greenbelt areas amid the development and sprawl of cities?

How do suburban areas tend to be segregated?

1   2

About what percentage of people live in suburbs instead of cities or rural area? _____

Suburbs offer their own kind of attractions- name some:

_____

For what reasons have businesses moved to suburbs?

_____

As people and businesses moved to suburbs, retailers have followed. Why?

_____

Malls _____

Car Congestion _____

Car Tolls _____

Car Permits _____

Car bans _____

Rush hour _____

Concerning transportation, America is an _____ *-dominated culture.*

Trace the phases of American urban development regarding transportation:

1	2	3
pedestrian phase	**streetcar phase**	**automobile phase**

_____

How have governments used fines on drivers to discourage traffic during peak hours?

1   2

3   4

Which of these methods do you 'agree most' with? _____

Public transportation _____

Diesel _____

Hybrid

Ethanol

Electric

Plug-in hybrid

Hydrogen fuel cell

What are the current developments regarding the following forms of public transport:

Trolleys	**Buses**	**Rapid transit**

European cities tend to have   **more**   **less**   *public transportation options than American cities.*

Filtering

Redlining

Public housing

Community Reinvestment Act

Housing Choice Voucher Program

Gentrification

Why do inner cities face distinctive challenges? Name some issues faced by people in inner cities in America:

What is the result of the process of filtering?

When urban renewal 'projects' were built in the 1960s-1980s, what was the point of them?	Why did they come to be criticized by the 1990s?

Underclass

Culture of poverty

Who builds and maintains most public housing?	What is a Housing Credit Voucher?

In the process of gentrification, what are the five reasons middle class people move back to urban neighborhoods and what is the effect?

1

2

3

4

5

Why has the process of gentrification, apparently a good thing for housing quality, been criticized (poststructuralism)?

How do the underclass problems in America compare with India?

What is a deadbeat dad?

How have cities dealt with the low income from tax revenues in urban neighborhoods?

1

2

What has been the effect on cities of the recession of 2008?

Cities are bouncing back- at least some of them are. What successes have the following cities had?

BOSTON	BALTIMORE	CHICAGO	NYC	SAN FRANCISCO

APPENDIX: MAP SCALE AND PROJECTIONS   NAME_____

Map scale _____

Word statement _____

Graphic scale _____

Representative fraction _____

Flattening _____

Conic _____

Cylindrical _____

Planar _____

Oval _____

Gnomonic projection _____

Layering _____

Peters projection* _____

Buckminster Fuller* _____

Dymaxion map* _____

_____

_____

_____

_____

_____

_____

_____

_____

Part II

Vocabulary Extras

VOCAB EXTRAS: TERMS FROM OTHER TEXTS:
USE QUIZLET TO GET UP TO SPEED WITH THESE TERMS

NAME_____

Phenomenon _____

Quantitative revolution _____

Four Traditions _____

Five Themes _____

Region as a concept _____

Qualitative data _____

Idiographic vs. nomothetic _____

Geoid _____

Resolution _____

Choropleth map _____

Power of maps _____

Deception of maps _____

Relative distance _____

Clustered _____

First Law of Geography _____

Connectivity _____

Accessibility

Spatial diffusion

Relocation/Stimulus/Contagious/Hierarchical diffusion

Barriers to diffusion: physical vs. sociocultural vs. psychological

Demographic accounting equation

Factors determining NIR: education, economics, cultural traditions, gender empowerment, policy

Wide base, small base, disrupted growth, rectangular population pyramids

Baby boom / baby bust

Overpopulation

Cornucopian

Cairo Plan

Sustainability

Internally displaced persons

Cultural complex

Sacred spaces (sites)

Interfaith vs. Intrafaith boundary

Cultural imperialism

---this space intentionally left empty---

Sense of place

Placelessness

Challenges to modern state

States' rights

Subsequent boundary

Relic boundaries

Antecedent boundary

Positional disputes

Territorial disputes

Functional disputes

Resource disputes

Cores

Peripheries

(4th generation) Sub-national identities

Separatism

Domino theory

Frontier

Land claims- Antarctica/Seas/Space

East-west divide

Geography of terrorism

Bride burning

Female infanticide

Necessity is the mother of invention

Carbon footprint

Epidemiological Transition Model

Eugenics/Dysgenics

Family planning

Holistic

Gendered space

Generation of little emperors

Generation X

Millennial

Grameen Bank

J-Curve/S-Curve

Maladaption

Optimum population

Polygamy

Positive correlation

Replacement rate

ZPG

Amnesty

Asylum

Cyclic migration

Immigration wave

Minutemen

Sanctuary city

Sphere (celestial) / (of Influence)

Conquest

Commodification

Cultural appropriation

Cultural extinction

Ethnosphere

Global-local continuum

Invasion-Succession

Dialect chains

Linguistic reconstruction

Language convergence and divergence

Ashkenazim / Sephardim

Feng Shui

Sharia

Organic theory

Peace of Westphalia

World Systems Theory

Contact zone

Semi-Periphery

Darfur

Carrot and stick

Meets and Bounds system

Long Lots system

Cadastral system

Township and range system

Auto Alley

Big box retailers

Happiness index

High tech corridor

Silicon valley

Wealth gap

Dependency theory

Growth poles

Multiplier effect

Venture capital

Fisheries depletion

Subsidies

Debt for nature swap

City beautiful movement

City of the dead

Empowerment zone

Entrepot

Electronic road pricing

Exurb

Gated community

Urban decay

New urbanism

Seaside, FL

Nucleated settlement

Peak land value intersection

Periferico

Post-Modern landscape

Structuralism

Modernism

Postmodernism

Poststructuralism

Feminism

Reviving CBDs

Joel Garreau

T.G. McGee

Lewis Mumford*

Jane Jacobs*

Addenda: Extra Resources

Crash Course Guide

Reviewer _____

It's Review Time!

Topic of today's episode _____

Preview: I think Hank Green will be talking about the following topics:

Some things I learned that were not in the book or talked about in class:

_____

What silly (or not so silly) gimmicks did Mr. Green have this time?

_____

How did those items or gimmicks tie-in to the material in the chapter?

_____

_____

_____

After Watching:

    a)   Was there a 'deep' lesson at the very end? What was it?

    b)   To me, the most interesting topic in this chapter, most relevant to my life, is _____ because:

_____

Travel Documentary

Traveler _____

Ch. 6: Religion – Israel & Palestine

Watching at home? Do a video search for: *Rick Steves Israel Palestine.*

Why is the 'Holy Land' holy to people of the following faiths:

1) Christians:

2) Muslims:

3) Jews:

Between the 1st and 20th centuries, the land was called _____

Jews became a majority with the creation of the State of _____ in 1948.

What happened after the 1947 Arab-Israeli War?

What happened after the 1967 Six-Days War?

Name three sacred spaces in the Old City of Jerusalem:

Describe some of the things Mr. Steves learns about in the Jewish areas:

Describe some impressions you have of the Palestinian areas:

Test Correction Guide

Time to get it right!

Corrector_____

Test Name_____

Directions: Identify the numbers of the answers you got wrong on the test and write them:

Number   **Page in Book**   **Correct answer (written in the form of a statement using stem of question)**

_____

_____

_____

_____

_____

_____

_____

_____

_____

_____

_____

_____

_____

_____

_____

_____

_____

_____

_____

_____

I got most of these wrong because…

Geo Movie Review

Reviewer _____

What chapter in the book is this movie most appropriate for? _____

The topic(s) it cover(s): _____

Identify some of the key characters in the movie that embody concepts in the chapter. Describe how the geographical issue(s) affect the storyline in the early part of the film.

_____

_____

_____

_____

What was the "low point" for the main character(s) in the movie? Did the geography issue cause that low point / crisis to occur?

_____

_____

By the end of the movie, it is probable that whatever crises or effects the geographical issue was causing was resolved in some way. Explain how this turn of events came about:

_____

_____

_____

Rate this movie from 0-3: _____
3: it was intellectually stimulating and entertaining
2: it had good points but was rather dull
1: it seemed misleading or irrelevant
0: it was not worth seeing- waste of time

One image or scene that stuck out was:

_____

_____

Why did you rate it the way you did?

_____

_____

Would you recommend this movie to Friends or relatives outside of geo class?

_____

_____

Geo Documentary Review

Reviewer _____

What chapter in the book is this documentary most appropriate for? _____

What topics does it cover? _____

According to the documentary, what was the previous status quo or situation, and how did it change? What implications does the documentary present for the future?

PAST　　　　　　　　　　　　　　**PRESENT**　　　　　　　　　　　　　　**FUTURE**

How does the material presented in this documentary help you understand the chapter? Describe briefly if you will think about things differently and how:

_____

_____

Rate this documentary from 0-3: _____
3: it was intellectually stimulating and informative
2: it had good points but was rather dull
1: it seemed misleading or irrelevant
0: it was not worth seeing- waste of time

Why did you rate it the way you did?

_____

_____

One image or scene that stuck out was:

_____

_____

Why do you think this particular scene was more memorable than the rest?

_____

_____

_____

Any final thoughts on this documentary?

APHUG: Language: "Darmok" Season 5 ep. 2
"Dathon & Picard at El'A'Drel"

The Importance of Language and Communication

Directions:

Read over the definitions before watching:

Standard language – a language substantially uniform with respect to spelling, grammar, pronunciation, and vocabulary and representing the approved community norm of the tongue.

Dialect – a language variant marked by vocabulary, grammar and pronunciation differences from other variants of the same common language. When those variations are spatial or regional, they are called geographic dialects; when they are indicative of socioeconomic or educational levels, they are called social dialects. For example, cockney which is the variation of the English language.

Pidgin – An auxiliary language derived, with reduced vocabulary and simplified structure, from other languages. Not a native tongue, it is used for limited communication between people with different languages, for purposes such as commerce, administration or work supervision. For example, Lingala, spoken by the 270 different ethnic groups of the Congo, to facilitate the recruitment of soldiers

Creole (ization) – A language developed from a pidgin to become the native tongue of a society. For example, Swahili.

Lingua Franca – Any of various auxiliary languages used as common tongues among people of an area where several languages are spoken; literally, "Frankish language." For example, a language of trade and travel.

Official language - A governmentally designated language of instruction, of government, of the courts, and other official public and private communication.

ENTERPRISE CREW:

JEAN LUC PICARD – CAPTAIN, Earth, "bald guy"
    WILLIAM RIKER – FIRST OFFICER, Earth, "beard guy"
        DEANNA TROI – SHIP'S COUNSELOR, Betazed, "telepathic"
            GEORDI LAFORGE – ENGINEER, Earth, "has visor"
                MR. DATA – SCIENCE OFFICER, Omicron III, "pasty android"
                    DR. BEVERLY CRUSHER – DOCTOR, Earth, "uses tricorder"
                        MILES O'BRIEN – TRANSPORTER TECH., earth
                            WORF – WEAPONS OFFICER, "#OnlyKlingon"

TAMARIAN ALIENS:

DATHON – CAPTAIN   ????????? – FIRST OFFICER

1. What is the immediate problem facing the Enterprise personnel and the Tamarians?

2. What happens to provoke the Enterprise and its crew?

3. How does the staff on the Enterprise deal with the provocation? Are they successful? Why/Why not?

4. How does Picard decide to deal with the provocation on the planet?

5. What changes do Dathon and Picard experience? How does this come about?

6. Why is the story of Gilgamesh important at the end of the film?

7. What implications do the events that occurred on El'A'Drel have for the Tamarians and the Federation to which the Enterprise personnel belong?

8. What does this video have to do with language and culture? Use terms from the chapter

9. What other branches of Human Geography might this film also be used to discuss (look at chapter titles!)

Questions associated with but not connected to this specific video:

1. What impact has the Internet had on communication? What is or are the lingua francas used on the Internet? Will these affect cultural identities in the future?

2. How have periods of colonization throughout history affected languages both positively and negatively?

Best Bets Online

All of the following are indexed for convenience at Antarcticaedu.com/Geo.htm

Kahoot.it can be a fun review game. Make a free account and the students can compete using their smartphones. Search for AP Human Geography jeopardy-style quizzes.

Many geography teachers put together good sites is a very good sites. Students can use them as a summary of the chapters in the text and for review.

Quizlet has a ton of vocab, and is a good way for students to get the stuff other books might have but the Rubenstein book does not have.

On CharlieRose.com, a famed interviewer talks to people working in geography (as well as most other fields) and you can search by topic.

Ted.com/talks has geography related speakers.

Yale University has open courses you can listen to about geographical and environmental topics and issues at Antarcticaedu.com/opencourses.htm

Look for City Journal magazine, with urban issues.

On Youtube, search for Crash Course for reviews, as well as the many clips suggested above and others. You can download the video if your school blocks Youtube, and bring the clips in on an external hard drive.

As Rubenstein is the most widely used textbook now, and has been for a generation, which textbooks were most popular two and three generations back? In the 1990s it was Harm de Blij's text. Old editions cost about 5 bucks on Amazon or Abebooks, and for perspective's sake are probably worth obtaining.

Note: Bookfinder.com will locate these titles for you if you would like to procure any of them. Addall.com has the same information and searching ability, but presents the results in a different order. Abebooks.com is good too, but it doesn't search Amazon.com like the others, despite being owned by Amazon.

350 Years of Geography Education

1600s

Nathanial Carpenter's *Geography Delineated Forth in Two Bookes* (1625) is the earliest book on the subject written in original English, but Peter Heylyn's vast *Cosmographie* (1652) may be the first usable textbook. Among other things, it contained the first detailed analysis of every world region and realm then known, including the Americas. While Australia and Antarctica were not present because they were not yet discovered, Heylyn had a solid 90 percent of the globe described in great detail. *Cosmographie* continued as a standard work into the 18th century, and was reprinted many times. Atlases appeared to complement it, the *Atlas Minimus* of John Seller being notable. Expanding on the work of German cartographer Martin Waldseemuller (who first used the term 'America' on a map) and Belgian cartographer Abraham Ortelius (who provided the world with its first modern atlas), Sellers' book of maps was reprinted every few years for a century- not a bad run.

Early-1700s

As the new century opened, Herman Moll brought out a competitor atlas called *A System of Geography* (1701), which also went through many editions, as did *Geography Anatomis'd* (1716) by Patrick Gordon, which appeared anew every few years into the 1750s. The atlas books did not go into the descriptive detail on all lands that *Cosmographie* did, but they had the maps, which are prized by collectors today. Furthermore, geography was a subject that was *usable*. Traders and merchants counted on geographic data, statesmen used it in their decision-making, and the growing military arms of modern governments required it for their actions. Germany was the leading nation in the subject, and that is where Johann Hubner published a geography book for classrooms, later translated as *A New and Easy Introduction to the Study of Geography by the Question and Answer Method* (1693). It was used in Britain into the 1760s.

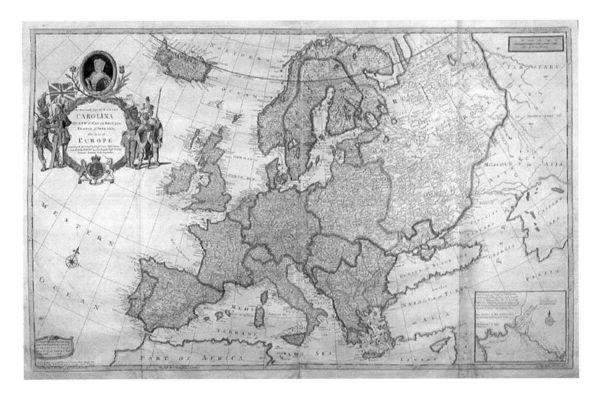

Moll's Map of Europe

When Isaac Watts, a famous writer of hymns, produced *Knowledge of the Heavens and the Earth Made Easy* (1726), his well-known stature helped make it a popular work for homes. It ran through many editions into the 1770s. Indeed, apart from world geographies, the three most oft appearing specific works on the subject were geographies of the heavens (which were really astronomy books), geographies of the British Empire specifically, and geographies of Palestine to accompany people's reading of the Bible. But the big story of the early-18th century for professionals was the 1733 translation of another great German work, *Geographia Generalis* by Bernhardus Varenius, under the title *A Complete System of General Geography* (1650). The English version had the additional distinction of being read, critiqued, and brought up to date by Isaac Newton himself. According to the *Encyclopedia Britannica*, "It dealt with the subject of geography in a truly philosophic spirit; and long held its position as the best treatise in existence on scientific and comparative geography."[1]

Late-1700s

These works were succeeded after a few decades by another German masterpiece, this one by Anton Friedrich Busching, called *Erdebeschreibung*. Literally *Earth Description*, this book was translated under the title *A New System of Geography* in 1754. Busching was renowned as a proponent of geography education. William Guthrie's *New System of Modern Geography* (1760) made the rounds for thirty years in England, and was revitalized by David Rittenhouse in the 1790s. Charles Middleton's *A New and Complete System of Geography* (1777), along with Richard Turner's *A New and Easy Introduction to Universal Geography* (1780), were the last textbooks to include the Thirteen American Colonies as a part of the British Empire. Turner's work would run into 13 editions, the last appearing in 1808.

Richard Gadesby's *A New and Easy Introduction to Geography* and George Millar's *A New and Compete System of Geography,* both published in 1783, saw some rounds in schools, while Thomas Salman's *Atlas* was a standard accompaniment. One geographer who never wrote a textbook was Immanuel Kant, mainly because he wrote books about every other subject. But we do know of his lectures in geography as professor at the University of Konigsberg, because for 30 years his students took notes. After Kant died it was clear he would write no geography book, and some enterprising knowledge fiends sought out his former charges and hacked their notebooks on what he said, compiled it all, and systematized the mess- something that should warm the heart of any teacher.

In 1789, two years after the Constitution was promulgated in Philadelphia but three years before it was fully ratified, Jedidiah Morse published *American Universal Geography* (1789), the first textbook on the subject to be used in the schools of the new nation, where it enjoyed a virtual monopoly for two decades. Nathanial Dwight brought out a complementary work for kids called *A Short but Comprehensive System of the Geography of the World: by Way of Question and Answer, Principally Designed for Children and Common Schools* (1796), which served as a preparatory work. In Britain, Nicholas Dufresnoy's *Geography for Children* (1797) assumed the role Dwight's did in America, while John Pinkerton's *Modern Geography* served British secondary schools into the 1820s. Morse's book was a runaway success. It was reprinted almost every year, as geographical changes were occurring fast. He became known as the 'Father of American Geography.' Twenty years on, it was time for Morse to bring out a totally new textbook, which he called *Geography Made Easy* (1811). In both works his method was to examine the states individually, as if they were countries, as road atlases depict them. This was done in the national history books as well, which mirrored the more intense state identities of average people before the Civil War.

---

[1] "Varenius, Bernhardus." 1911. *Encyclopedia Britannica.* Cambridge University Press.

1800s

As the 19th century began, Susanna Rowson prepared a textbook especially for use in girls' schools. Called *An Abridgement of Universal Geography* (1805), this book was part of Rowson's wide-ranging series of school materials, which included spelling books, reading books on civics such as *The Female Patriot* (1795) and *Columbian Daughters* (1800), Bible dialogues, and a history book. She did for women's geography what Emma Willard did for women's history and science. Other books which appeared briefly were Elijah Parish's *Compendium of Universal Geography Designed for Schools* (1807), and Sir Richard Phillips' *Elements of Geography: Compiled from the Latest European and American Travelers, Voyagers and Geographers* 1807). The subtitle of the latter reminds us how quickly new information was being brought in as the remainder of the big globe's contours were being surveyed. Phillips, meanwhile, was knighted in Britain for his dedication and work in academics and democratizing knowledge. He provided a strategy for using his work in the preface:

"The proper mode of using this little book to advantage will be to direct the pupil to commit the whole of the facts to memory, at the rate of one, two, or three, per day, according to age and capacity; taking care, at the end of each section, to make him repeat the whole of what he has before learnt."[2]

Good advice to relay at your next parent-teacher conference. Next up we have the Rev. J. Goldsmith, who produced *An Easy Grammar of Geography* (1803), which had a half-century run, being revised into the 1850s. E.G. Spafford's *General Geography* (1809) is possibly the only textbook to use the term Fredonia as a synonym for the United States. Benjamin Davies' *A Short and Easy Introduction to Universal Geography* (1810) went through a few revisions and releases, and Joseph Guy's *School Geography* (1810) was so respected it continued to be released by his kinsfolk and the publishers even after his death.

1810s

Historical geography, as separate from physical and human, was gaining momentum with Jacob Cummings' *An Introduction to Ancient and Modern Geography on the Plan of Goldsmith and Guy* (1813), and Samuel Butler's *A Sketch of Modern and Ancient Geography* (1813). Butler was one of the great schoolmasters of early-Victorian England. Educated at the famous Rugby School and then at Cambridge, where he won scholarships for essays in Latin, he became headmaster of Shrewsbury School, where he "raised the standard of its scholarship to the equal of any other public school in England."[3] Butler originated the *Praposter* system of placing older boys in authority over younger ones at the school. A notable pupil of his was Charles Darwin, though Darwin didn't much care for Butler's insistence on rote learning.

Rodolphus Dickenson's *Elements of Geography* (1813) came next, while Christopher Kelly's multivolume *A New and Complete Sketch of Universal Geography*, E. Mackenzie's *A New and Complete System of Geography*, and Daniel Adams' *Geography, or, A Description of the World*, all appeared in 1816 and went through multiple editions. The end of the decade saw the publication of Joseph Worcester's *Elements of Geography* (1819) which ran clear into the 1840s, being revised every five years or so. Worcester was a famous lexicographer, a person who systematizes words and their vocabulary meanings, and was chief rival to Noah Webster in the 'Dictionary Wars.' He was one of those who, like Alfred Russel Wallace, simultaneously reached the same conclusion or invention but was a day late and a dollar short. You might say he was the second definition in the dictionary under 'lexicographer.' But this is no mean accomplishment- had Alexander Graham Bell not made it to the

---

[2] Marsden, William. 2001. *The School Textbook: History, Geography and Social Studies.* Routledge.
[3] "Butler, Samuel." 1911. *Encyclopedia Britannica.* Cambridge University Press.

patent office when he did, he would have been on this list because Thomas Edison was right on his heels- and would have gotten the telephone patent to add to his mountain of others.

1820s

Jedidiah Morse was not only the father of American geography; he was also an actual father to two notable sons. Samuel would go on to invent Morse code for the telegraph, used between 1844 and 1999, which saved countless lives out at sea by giving stranded sailors the ability to relay the simple distress call: SOS. The other son, Sidney, followed in his father's footsteps and become a geographer. He invented cerography, an early method of printing color maps in textbooks. Sidney released *A New System of Geography* (1823) with his cerographic color maps, a book that was actually in competition with his father's during the middle part of the decade. Both sold well, and over time, half a million copies of Sidney's book made their way into schools and homes.

William C. Woodbridge's *Rudiments of Geography* was also used at this juncture, appearing in 1825 and going through successive additions. In Canada, Walter Bromley's *Catechism of Geography Adapted to Every Age and Capacity, and to Every Class of Learners, in either Ladies or Gentleman's Schools* (1825), also made its appearance, without any attempt to hid who its target audience might be. A year later, as he lay on his deathbed *ala* Copernicus, Danish geographer Malte Conrad Brun's *Universal Geography* was printed. Too large for use in schools, it instantly became the standard for professionals of the mid-19th century. Brun's story is a little quixotic. A liberal in a monarchic age, he left Denmark because of political disagreements, went to France, and altered the spelling of his name to something that would surely fool the Pink Panther's ancestors: Conrad Malte-Brun, the name by which he is known today.

The debut year for another of the big names in geography education came shortly thereafter. Samuel Griswold Goodrich (aka Peter Parley) released *Outlines of Modern Geography* (1827), a highly popular work later revised into *A System of School Geography*. Goodrich, a Massachusetts State Senator, summarized the 6-volume work of Malte-Brun into something more digestible by students, and his textbooks would become the most used for decades to come. British works appearing during the 1820s were James Bell's *A System of Geography* (1828), Ingram Cobbin's *Elements of Geography on a New Plan, Rendered Plain and Amusing, More Especially Adapted to the Capacities of Young Children and Designed for Preparatory Schools* (1828), and Thomas Ewing's *A System of Geography for the Use of Schools and Private Students* (1828). Bell's work had a multi-decade run. Also in 1828, James Olney brought out an atlas to use with other texts, then dropped the pretense and produced his own whole book: *Practical System of Modern Geography, or, a View of the Present State of the World* (1831), which ran for about 15 years. Nathan Hale's *Epitome of Universal Geography* (1830) was aimed at university students.

1830s

As the new decade broke, Goodrich put out an atlas called *The Universal School Atlas, Arranged on the Inductive Plan, and Designed to Render the Study of Geography Both Easy and Instructive* (1832). He then turned to the needs of youngsters, producing a whimsical pseudonym called Peter Parley, and having 'him' write *Peter Parley's Method of Telling about Geography to Children, Principally for the Use of Schools* (1832). While Goodrich exchanged political and literary letters with John Adams, H.W. Longfellow, Thomas Hart Benton, Winfield Scott, Washington Irving, Victor Hugo, Horace Greely, Alexis de Tocqueville and other luminaries, Parley found some competition as 1833 dawned. That year marked the appearance of John J. Clute's highly regarded *School Geography* (1833), and soon after came J.L. Blake's *American Universal Geography for Schools and Academies* (1834), which upped the ante even more. After that Roswell Smith put out a popular and recommendable two-volume textbook called *Geography on the Productive System* (1835), which would run through successive editions for the next 40 years. But Peter Parley had the lion's share of the market. The pseudonym was so popular that street names can be found today with *Parley's* name on them in the northeast of America!

In Edinburgh at the time, Alexander Stewart's *Compendium of Modern Geography* (1835) featured exam questions at the end of each chapter, an early version of the 'section review' that students look forward to so. It had a 20-year run. After these debuted, Thomas Smiley's *An Easy Introduction to the Study of Geography, on an Improved Plan Compiled for the Use of Schools* (1836), and Nathanial Gilbert Huntington's *Introduction to Modern Geography for Beginners and Common Schools* (1838) appeared. Meanwhile in London, Aaron Arrowsmith, founder of a great mapmaking family, who had been producing atlases for Samuel Butler's textbooks for twenty years, came out with a textbook of his own, called *A Compendium of Ancient and Modern Geography* (1839). His work targeted Eton and King's College students.

1840s

In the 1840s, new versions of old favorites continued to hold the market. Goodrich took a break from government to produce new textbooks. First, there was *Pictorial Geography of the World* (1840), then *A National Geography for Schools* (1845). New editions of Samuel Butler's work appeared in Britain, and Sidney Morse's *System of Geography* continued its long and influential run in America. A new face on the scene was that of Samuel Augustus Mitchell, who quickly became a leading force in geography education with *Mitchell's Geographic Reader: A System of Modern Geography* (1840). A few years later he added to this influence with *An Easy Introduction to the Study of Geography* (1843), and *Mitchell's Primary Geography* (1845). His school atlas is a classic of the period as well. Back in Britain, education magnate James Cornwell was already well known for his series of Victorian schoolbooks, and now he branched into the social studies with *A School Geography* (1840), which ran through many editions. A shorter-lived book that ran about a decade was Sylvester Bliss' *Analysis of Geography for use of Schools and Academies* (1847).

In the professional field, Alexander von Humboldt's magisterial *Kosmos,* translated from German to English as *Cosmos* (1845), electrified the field of consideration by the collective geographic mind. Humboldt attempted to delineate the natural universe and describe man's place within it after a lifetime of study, often firsthand, in places no European had ever set foot. He marched through the tropics, through Siberia, and finally, according to the translator, "felt rich enough in knowledge and materials to reduce into form and reality the unrefined vision that floated before him." Humboldt himself described this vision in detail:

"In the late evening of an active life, I offer to the German public a work whose completion I have frequently looked to as impracticable. But I was occupied for many years with an irresistible impulse. It was the earnest endeavor to comprehend the phenomena of physical objects in their general connexion, and to represent nature as a great whole, moved an animated by internal forces... My aim was to begin with the depths of space, in the regions of the remotest nebulae, and gradually descend through the starry zone to which our solar system belongs, down to our own terrestrial spheroid, encircled by air and ocean, there to direct attention to its form, temperature and magnetic tension, and to consider the fullness of organic life unfolding upon its surface, beneath the vivifying influence of light."[4]

In a class by himself, Humboldt was so well regarded that 10 American states- and as many countries from Peru to Germany- have cities and counties named after him. Thomas Jefferson said, "I consider Humboldt the most important scientist I have ever met." Edgar Allan Poe dedicated his last poem to Humboldt. Simon Bolivar said, "The real discoverer of South America was Humboldt, since his work was more useful for our people than the work of all conquerors," while Charles Darwin told Humboldt

---

[4] Humboldt, Alexander von. 1845. *Cosmos.* Harper & Bros.

in a letter that it was his book that inspired him to undertake that fateful voyage aboard the HMS Beagle, into the torrid zones of the earth.[5]

Before this decade was out, *Black's General Atlas* (1846) was released- a notable work because it featured the maps of John Bartholomew, head of the great mapmaking family of Scotland, which is still doing cartography after two centuries. Today HarperCollins owns the old firm, but Bartholomew's descendants run it.

1850s

With these changes and others in mind, in the early-1850s the Mitchell, Goodrich, Goldsmith, Smith, Olney and Butler texts all appeared in new editions, and were holding strong in the academic marketplace. Some now had the atlases inside the textbooks instead of apart, but most students still had to negotiate with two books. One notable addition to the lot was Francis McNally's *An improved system of geography: Designed for schools, academies and seminaries* (1855). Samuel Maunder's *Treasury of Geography* (1856) appeared too, as part of a textbook series all having 'Treasury' in the name (for example *Treasury of History* was used in history classes, etc.). Guy's textbook was reprinted in 1856, while E.E. White's *A Class-Book of Geography Containing a Complete Syllabus of Oral Instruction on the Method of Object Teaching; also, Map Exercises, Systematically Arranged for Class Drill* (1856) contained a full testing program. S.S. Cornell came out with a series the same year, consisting of three books: *Cornell's Primary Geography*, *Cornell's Intermediate Geography* and *Cornell's High School Geography*. S.S. stood for Sarah Sophia, who followed the common practice of hiding the fact she was a woman by using her initials. She brought out an atlas to go with this series, which appeared under the title *Cornell's Companion Atlas to Cornell's High School Geography- comprising a complete set of maps, designed for the student to memorize, together with numerous maps for reference, etc.* (1861). Man or woman, textbook writers of the time didn't leave much to the imagination in naming their books.

1860s

During the Civil War years, the general trend was much the same as in the 1850s. Old favorites were all being republished, specifically, the textbooks of Goodrich, Smith, Cornell, Mitchell, Morse and Guy. Goodrich had three titles out during the decade, notably a deluxe reprinting of *Pictorial Geography of the World* (1861), containing 1,000 engravings. To these were added some new titles such as Alex Keith Johnston's *School Atlas of General and Descriptive Geography* (1860), and G. Woolworth Colton's *School Atlas* (1860). Gazetteers were becoming popular in the general public, and were often brought into schools too. Blackie's *Imperial Gazetteer* from Britain is probably the best example. Canadian geographers under George Hodgins got together to produce *Lovell's School Atlas* (1861), part of a series of schoolbooks put out by the firm, which advertised itself in the following way: "It may be proper to state here that an entirely new series of maps has been constructed at great expense for this Geography by draftsmen in Canada."[6] The book contained a total of 43 maps, and is a good example of a rare and expensive antique geography book, due to the parting out of the atlas (like with old car parts, the individual maps of old atlases sold separately are usually worth more than the atlas as a whole). George Perkins Marsh's *Man and Nature, or Physical Geography as Modified by Human Action* (1864), published by Scribner, was an influential academic work that helped begin the conservationist line of thought Teddy Roosevelt would appreciate when he set aside land for national parks.

After the Civil War, James Monteith contributed much to geographic literacy. He brought out a whole series of textbooks with state-specific addendums, knowing that in the USA, each individual state and locality was responsible for providing the whole course of education to their citizens. There was- and is-

---

[5] "Humboldt, Alexander von." 1911. *Encyclopedia Britannica 11th ed.* Cambridge University Press.
[6] Hodgins, George. 1861. *Lovell's School Atlas.* Lovell's.

no national curriculum, and back then, there was no Federal Department of Education. Thus, curriculum reflected local attitudes, which was more democratic because local educators and officials made the basic decisions and outlined guiding principles. First off, Monteith set out a standard, universal curriculum for primary schools in *Monteith's First Lessons in Geography on a Plan of Object Teaching* (1862). Then, as students got older, they would get the specific one for their state. If one's school adopted Monteith's *Manual of Geography, Combined with History and Astronomy; Designed for Intermediate Classes in Public and Private Schools* (1862), or his *Comprehensive Geography,* they would get a New York version, Pennsylvania version, Michigan version, etc. In 1868 he brought out a 'Pacific Coast' version, the first of its kind. Monteith's books became widely used throughout the country, and over the course of the decade began to supplant older favorites like Goodrich and Parley (both of whom died in 1860), and Mitchell (who died in 1868), though Mitchell's texts would continue to be revised and released. Monteith shared the field with McNally, Cornell and others, including Samuel Butler's half-century old classic, which was now being revised and edited by his son: John Olding Butler.

During the late-1860s, continental European methods and style were emphasized in books for the English-speaking world. Swiss geologist Arnold Henry Guyot, a leader in university geology at the time, tried his hand at popularizing geology through geography texts with *The Earth and Its Inhabitants: Common-School Geography* (1866). Just after that, Thomas Sedgwick Fay's *Great Outline Of Geography For High Schools And Families* (1867) specifically wove European advancements into the American curriculum. The book was Fay's swansong after a three-decade long career representing America in Europe as a diplomat. In Britain, Robert Anderson's series made its appearance, starting with *Modern Geography* (1863). His books would appear for over two decades, as would those of D.M. Warren, who began his stint with *The Common-School Geography: An Elementary Treatise on Mathematical, Physical and Political Geography* (1868). John Miller Dow Meiklejohn's *On the Best & the Worst Methods of Teaching Geography, A Short Lecture to Schoolmasters* (1869) contained advice to teachers from a noted British professor who, decades earlier at the age of 20, translated Immanuel Kant's *Critique of Pure Reason* into English. Why? He had his reason(s).

1870s

During the 1870s, Germany was still the world-center of geography teaching. In the year 1875 alone, ten universities started geography departments by the royal decree of Kaiser Wilhelm I. Holland also began a geography department at the University of Amsterdam, which focused on the colonial Dutch East Indies- sea routes to get there, the islands themselves, and the their physical and human features. And the textbooks kept rolling out. Mitchell's venerated geography was still being revised and released, along with about ten of the books already mentioned, including the McNally text, now under the imprint *National Geographical Series: An Improved System of Geography* (1872).

New books included *A School Geography: Embracing a Mathematical, Physical, and Political Descriptions of the Earth* (1870) by Adolf von Steinwehr, a German immigrant who led an infantry unit of fellow German immigrants from New York during the Civil War. He led them at the battle of Bull Run, and later commanded units at Chancellorsville and Gettysburg against Stonewall Jackson, which is ironic because of what the name 'Steinwehr' means in German. It means 'stone barrier,' specifically, one in a river that changes or obstructs the flow of its water. At one point, therefore, we had Stone Wall squaring off against Stone Weir. Who knew? A kindred work was the New Brunswick Series' *School Geography of the World* (1872), written by J. B. Calkins. On the purely physical side of things, noted diplomat Viscount James Bryce put out *The Student's Atlas of Physical Geography* (1873), and Guyot brought out *Physical Geography* (1873).

In the latter part of the decade, George Gill's *Imperial Geography for College and School Use* (1875) appeared on the scene and was used in Britain, along with the work of academic William Swinton, whose *Elementary Course in Geography* (1875) and *Complete Course in Geography* (1876) were well regarded. Other works from Britain included *The Royal School Series Geography and Atlas,* published by T. Nelson every few years. Harper's got in on the action as well, releasing *Harper's School Geography with Maps and Illustrations Prepared Expressly for this Work by Eminent American Artists* (1876). Finally, William Hughes produced *A Class-Book of Modern Geography with Examination Questions* (1879). This book was a bit large for some classrooms, so a few years later Francon Williams abridged and re-released it.

1880s

During the 1880s, Swinton, Johnston, McNally, Warren, Steinwehr, Colton, the Harper's series, Guyot, Monteith, Goldsmith, Anderson, Guy, Cornwell and Mitchell were all still in the game. Appleton's came out with an educational series called *Appleton's American Standard Geographies* (1880), aimed at different levels and featuring *Standard Higher Geography* (1881) for secondary schools. The business of publishing review books came into being when the New York Regent's Exam began carrying a geography section. In response to this, the Bulletin Press of New York released the questions from the first exam- over a decade late but better late than never- as *The Regent's Questions from the First Examination in Geography* (1880). Such volumes would appear sporadically to, in some sense, this very day.

Other books appeared as well. There was the *School Manuel of Modern Geography* (1880) by J. Richardson, and George F. Cram appeared on the scene with his *Illustrated Handbook of Geography* (1881). The quality of Cram's works is reflected well enough in the longevity of his later globe and mapmaking firm. Another big name in the subject, Professor Carl Ritter of the University of Berlin, published *Comparative Geography* (1881). It looked at how various interconnected phenomena influence places, and most argue he began the regional approach to the subject, in contrast to Humboldt's systematic approach. Edwin Houston started a multi-decade book too, *Elements of Physical Geography for the Use of Schools, Academies and Colleges* (1882), while the American Book Company put out a very nice text called *The Eclectic Complete Geography* (1883), which did not list the author's name but the authors were Steinwehr and D.G. Brinton. It included lessons for map drawing as well.

In 1887, Jacques Redway teamed with the Butler publishing company to produce *Butler's Compete Geography,* not to be confused with the now 70-year-old British work by Samuel Butler, a similarity that may have factored into naming the latter-day work that way. Either way, Redway's series would soon evolve into one of the most used geographies at the turn of the century, after it was purchased and marketed by the American Book Company, which learned well from Monteith's success in bringing out state-specific editions and did the same thing. In Canada, D.A. Chase released *High School Geography* (1887), which had to compete with the Department of Education's *The Public School Geography- Authorized for Use in the Public schools, High schools, and Collegiate Institutes of Ontario* (1887). Talk about a state education! Down under in Australia, A. Buckley put out *Class Book of Geography* (1888), while Sir Edward Strickland told everyone why it was worthwhile to study the subject in his *The Importance of Geography* (1888). At the end of the decade, John Duncan Quackenbos targeted kids with *Lessons in Geography for Little Learners* (1889), while teachers got a boon from Charles F. King's *Methods and Aids in Geography for the Use of Teachers and Normal Schools* (1889), and Redway's *The Teacher's Manual of Geography* (1889). To round things out, Meiklejohn, who previously issued his advice to teachers, now issued them a textbook: *A New Geography on the Comparative Method* (1889), which ran successfully till World War I.

1890s

In the 1890s, publishing houses captured most of the textbook market. George C. Chrisholm edited *Longman's School Geography* (1893) to compete with the Appleton and Harper lines, along with

Monteith, whose produce was rebranded The Barnes Series, after a publisher of that name seeking to attach successful titles to its mark. A year later Rand McNally brought out its own series, the *Rand McNally Primary School Geography* (1894) by James A. Bowen, and then expanded further with the release of *Grammar School Geography* (1894) by Woodward and Tiernan. Another company to produce a series was Werner, which released *Werner's Grammar School Geography: The World in Map and Picture* (1896) by Horace Tarbell. Sometimes the same company had multiple series running at the same time, as happens today. The American Book Company had that distinction. It already had Steinwehr and Brinton's *New Eclectic Complete Geography* out, but then it also bought up the Harper's series, and on top of that, it contracted Redway to team up with Russell Hinman to produce *Natural Advanced Geography* (1898), which took the market by storm at the turn of the century. This high quality series was probably the most used geography of the time.

Aside old reliable names like Anderson, Gill, Guyot, Hughes, Mitchell, Redway, and Swinton, some new faces, as usual, appeared. Alex Everett Frye is notable for *Frye's Complete Geography* (1895), which also came out in state-specific editions. H.O. Arnold-Forster got pesonal with his title, *This World of Ours: An Introduction to the Study of Geography* (1895), and Robert Sullivan in Britain maintained *Geography Generalised, an Introduction on the Principles of Classification and Comparison* (1896). Lionel Lyde took a different take with *Man and his Markets: A Course in Geography* (1896). William Sadlier's *Excelsior Geography* (1896) targeted Catholic students. Teachers were treated to *The Geography Class: How to Interest it* (1897) by Ida Dean. Andrew Herbertson released *An Illustrated School Geography* (1898), which contributed to his illustrious career as an educator focusing on regional study, while Whittaker & Co. and Oliver and Boyd's in London released two new geographies simultaneously, in direct competition with each other. Whittaker put out Charles Bird's *School Geography* (1898) and O&B released James Clyde's: *A School Geography* (1898).

Geographer John Keane, who contributed to other works in the past but never wrote a textbook, rounded out the century by analyzing the history of the subject in an interesting treatise called *The Evolution of Geography* (1899). Harvard geologist William Morris Davis' *Physical Geography* (1899) argued for environmental determinism as its main theme, and there may be no better exposition on the subject in English. As far as capstone volumes, H.R. Mill in Britain edited a thousand page tome called *The International Geography* (1899), which featured the collective work of seventy professionals writing on their subjects of expertise. But more than anything else, this was the age of the lavish, multi-volume ethnography, ancestor subject of cultural geography and to some extent, anthropology and sociology. In a semi-romantic way, explorers, missionaries, conquistadors, cartographers, settlers and mercantilists from Europe had been collecting data on all the world's people for centuries, and for the first time in history, descriptions of every group in the world could be portrayed in a book. This kind of observation and analysis is done in cultural geography and sociology all the time, but the late-19th century was a unique time to do it because modern culture had not yet descended upon the face of the world. There was, therefore, a short window in which worldwide ethnographies could be compiled on diverse human groups in at least a partly aboriginal state, and they were.

First came renowned French geographer Elisee Reclus' bombastic *Universal Geography: The Earth and its Inhabitants* (1878), rendered in a total of 19 luxury volumes. While it covered the known world with pictures and text, don't go looking for it unless you're ready to drop upwards of a thousand dollars. Although with today's textbooks selling for a hundred dollars each and more, maybe these volumes are worth ten copies of whatever is collecting dust in the school stock room? Hear the little voice in your head, "Priorities… priorities…" Additionally, Reclus' series was edited in English by E.G. Ravenstein, noted for his theory of migration, and by Augustus Henry Keane, noted philologist and later author of *Ethnology* (1896), published by Cambridge University Press. In 1920, Ellsworth Huntington advised his students, "Reclus' *Earth and Its Inhabitants* is unparalleled in interest and in the power of stimulating thought."[7] Reclus was an anti-government anarchist, which may sound humorous if one were writing something as state-related as a massive geography set, but in an article on the matter in *The American Conservative* (2010), Kirkpatrick Sale writes:

"For all [his] hatred of the status quo and desire for an end to the evils of capitalism, [Reclus] had nothing intentionally to do with bomb-throwers or assassins. He also had no taste for going around stirring up terrorists and in fact was busy writing his multi-volume Universal Geography, *an examination of every continent and country in terms of the effects that geographic features like rivers and mountains had on human populations- and vice versa... His geographical work, thoroughly researched and unflinchingly scientific, laid out a picture of human-nature interaction that we today would call bioregionalism. It showed, with more detail than anyone but a dedicated geographer could possibly absorb, how the ecology of a place determined the kinds of lives and livelihoods its denizens would have and thus how people could properly live in self-regarding and self-determined bioregions without the interference of large and centralized governments that always try to homogenize diverse geographical areas."*[8]

After Reclus came Cassell's *The World: Its Cities and Peoples* (c. 1885) in nine decorated volumes, the first three covering cities and the latter six covering peoples. Like Reclus, its format was regional, starting with Eskimos and moving down to the Northwest American Indians, the Indians of California, Indians of the Central Plains such as the Comanche and Apache, Pueblo Indians, Plain and Prairie Tribes such as the Utes and Pawnees, Indians of the Northeast such as the Delaware, Cherokee, Choctaw and other tribes of the Indian Territory, Canadian Indians like the Ojibway, Mexican and Central American Indians like the Aztecs and Mosquitians, South American Indians such as the Caribs, Arawaks, Waraus and Acawoios, Brazilian Indians, Bolivian and Pampean Indians, Chileno-Patagonians, Tierra del Fuegians, Peruvians, and finally Hispano-Americans. Off to the Pacific it was after that, and the next volumes continue with the Polynesians, Papuans, Australians, Tasmanians, Malays, Formosans and Malagasy tribes, then its on to the Middle East and Africa to visit the Aramaens, Abyssinians, Bedouins, Jews, Arabs, Egyptians, Berbers, Nilotic peoples, Kaffirs, Hottentots, Bushmen, Central African Negroes, West African Negroes such as the Ashanti, Dahomey tribes, Egbas, Gaboon tribes, Camma, Ishogos, Krumen, Angolese, Congolese, and Mandingos, then it is back to Asia to see the Persians, Kruds, Baluchi, Afghans, Paropamisans, Indians such as the Bheels, Warali, Meria, Kathkuri, Todas, Hindoos, Sikhs, and Singhalese, then Maldives islanders, Tibetans, Hill Tribes of Assam, Burmese, Siamese, Chinese, Manchus, Tartars, Turanians, Mongolians, Tungusians, Turks, Ugrians, Samoyedes, Yenesians, Lapps, Finns, Koreans, Loo-Choos, and Japanese, before moving towards Europe to pay a call to the Circassians, Mizadzhedzhi, Georgians, Lesgians, Magyars, Gypsies, Iberians, Basques, Aryans, Celts, Irish, Gaels, Manxmen, Welsh, Cornishmen, Bretons, Italics, Italians, Camorra, Neapolitans, Corsicans, Sardinians, Maltese, 'Italia Irredenta,' French, Spaniards, Portuguese, Rumanians, Swiss, Hellenics, Slavs, Russians, Illyrians, Servians, Croats, Montenegrins, Bulgarians, Lechs, Czechs, Letts, Lithuanians, Germanics, Frisians, Germans, Dutch, Scandinavians, and finally the English, about whom it concludes, "Stolid, as a rule, he is as impulsive as any Celt. Gifted with an unequalled capacity for self-government, he is ready, at the call of a party leader, to put into commission that power of thinking and deciding for himself, which has been the secret of his liberty."[9]

A few years later, Cassell's published a companion series focusing specifically on women's issues around the world, entitled *Women of All Nations: An Enthralling Pictorial Story of Womankind the World Over, A Record of Their Habits, Types of Beauty, Social Status, Marriage Customs and Influence* (1908). T. Athol Joyce, President of the Royal Anthropological Institute authored it, along with N.W.

---

[7] Huntington, Ellsworth. 1920. *Principles of Human Geography.* John Wiley.
[8] http://www.theamericanconservative.com/articles/are-anarchists-revolting/
[9] Various Authors. c. 1885. *The World Its Cities and Peoples.* Cassell's & Company Limited.

Thomas. For his later service in WWI, Joyce would be decorated with the Order of the British Empire. He spent time in Mexico excavating Mayan ruins with his wife.

In Germany, Friedrich Ratzel's celebrated *Volkerkunde* (1888) was translated into English as *The History of Mankind* (1896) in three volumes. In all likelihood the major ethnographical work that has ever been produced, Razel applied the evolutionary concept to all the societies and cultures of the world, and came up with the theory of *lebensraum*, the idea that the habitat in which one's nation lives influences its overall social destiny because it encourages or discourages the possibility of various human activities. Once a nation successfully masters its realm, it will seek to expand naturally if its population growth is above replacement. This is why, along with Herbert Spencer, Ratzel was marginalized after WWII for ideological reasons (Spencer formulated the theory of social darwinism in sociology, the concept in which societies can be seen as competing for territory on the world stage in the struggle for existence, as organisms do in nature). Amazingly, Ratzel's other major work, *Anthropogeographie*, has still never been translated into English.

John Clark Ridpath's *Great Races of Mankind: An Account of the Ethnic Origin, Primitive Estate, Early Migrations, Social Evolution, and Present Conditions and Promise of the Principal Families of Men* (1893), in eight volumes, followed suit, taking the reader on an ethnographic tour of the world. These large works of cultural geography reflected the increasing popularity of the subject. This popularity was also reflected in America at the University of California at Berkeley, which in 1898 became the first to establish a separate Department of Geography within its College of Commerce. From this center, California state normal schools (teacher education colleges) became staffed with geographers who brought the subject to work with them, increasing its presence on the academic landscape. This is why a rare document called *A Teacher's Handbook in Geography* (1905) is so interesting. Searchable only online because there were limited copies printed (which didn't stop Google from digitizing it), this document contains specific advice to teacher candidates from Walter J. Kenyon, Supervisor of Geography at the San Francisco State Normal School. Kenyon gave advice about North and South America, while Frank Buckner, also of the State Normal School, gave advice on Eurasia, Africa, Australia and the Islands of the Pacific. Together, they provide a treasure trove of strategies, structure, organization and method used in schools a century ago.

1900s

How many 19th century textbooks would continue successfully into the 20th? Quite a few came through, actually, starting with Redway and Hinman's *Natural Advanced Geography*, the most widely used textbook in America. Calkins' book was in; Houston's physical geography was in, celebrating its 20th anniversary with a reprinting. Hughes was in, Longman's series was in, Meiklejohn was in, Mitchell was in, Steinwehr was in, and Tarbell was in. Monteith and others faded out, as Goodrich and Morse did before. Frye's previous book was revised and released as *A Grammar School Geography* (1902), reviewed in Volume 1 of a new British periodical called *The Geographical Teacher*:

"Excellent though this book is in almost every respect, it is hardly likely to obtain much vogue in England or the simple reason that, though styled a 'general edition,' it is to all intents and purposes still an American- in its narrow sense of United States of America- volume. As to the book itself, we are already familiarized with its workings, its pictures, and many of its maps by Dr. Herbertson's capital edition of Frye's Illustrated School Geography. *The main drawback to its use in school is the unwieldy size and shape. The average schoolboy finds his school atlas awkward enough. What will he do with, and how will he find desk room for this gigantic* confrere, *measuring 12 by 19½ ins. and weighing nearly 3 lbs.? Passing by this physical difficulty, we have nothing but admiration for the book."*[10]

---
[10] A.W. Andrews and A.J. Herbertson. 1902. "The Geographical Teacher Vol. 1, No. 2." *The Geographical Association.*

Additionally, Frye's new book had misnamed three mountains in Canada. The maps had the old names, which the reviewers took issue with. In elementary education, new works appeared as well. First there was *World Pictures* (1902), written by J.B. Reynolds and published by A&C Black. The *TGT* reviewers were ambivalent about it:

"The book is described as an 'Elementary Pictorial Geography,' and the pictures are, therefore, the main point of the book, and they are for the most part good and illustrative and typical. They vary, of course, especially in the printing. The first one (Ben Nevis and Fort William) is poor compared with the second (Landing Stage, Glasgow); the drawing of the Chinamen in the tea plantation on pg. 77 irresistibly reminds one of the figures which embellish architectural plans and advertisements... What, however, constitutes a puzzle to us is the age of the 'children' for whom the book is meant. That they are quite young is evident from the preface, from the pictures, and from the type of questions asked; and yet the letterpress of the text and the quotations are surely over the heads of the little folk who will be 'introduced' to geographical study, who are to have their 'interest awakened,' and who are to 'feel their curiosity and imagination stimulated' (preface). They are told to read Westward Ho!, *Scott's poems, Longfellow's* Evangeline *&c., at the same time their teachers are warned off giving them political details until they have obtained a general impression of the chief natural areas of the Earth's surface. We may be wrong, but there seems some discrepancy here which might easily be obviated by simplifying through the language and style of the text."*[11]

Another series, this one for youngsters, was *Youth's Companion Series* (1902), published by Ginn under a variety of authors, about which the reviewers had the following to say:

"According to the prefatory note, these volumes 'provide in interesting and attractive form a supply of reading material for either home or school that is especially suitable for supplementing the formal reading of geography.' If the words 'or school' had been omitted, we should not have had a word to say against the books. The illustrations are good, the thumb-nail sketches in the margins clever, the style is pretty, witty, and undeniably interesting; but the whole 'facies,' as the botanists would say, is that of a series of magazine articles- excellent articles- but not suitable for young readers. Older boys, or girls, would make short work of the small pages of large print, while their younger brothers and sisters would hardly appreciate them. Here are two samples, No. 1 from Under Sunny Skies:

'How long ago did the Sultan make this garden for his love? I do not remember how many hundred years have passed since the dark-eyed beauty gathered its first roses, but still they freight the soft wind with their breath, and still the fairy ferns grow green, and the oranges ripen in the sun, and the solemn old carp are happy in the fish-pool; and I audaciously pluck the roses that are the far off descendants of those of that long past time, and the Sultana never heeds my trespass. She is as dead as Cordova.'

A really pretty bit of writing, but not specially adapted to supplement in school the formal teaching of geography. Again, No. 2 from Toward the Rising Sun:

'Once I inquired of an old man who cowered under the lee of a temple wall to escape the bitter wind of a December afternoon how far it was to a city which he named and where I hoped to pass the night. 'I don't know,' was the response. 'But don't you live here?' I asked. 'Yes; I've lived here just yonder all my life.' 'How old are you?' 'Seventy-four.' 'Then how can it be that you don't know the distance to Huailai?' 'How should I know? I have never been there.' The distance was eight miles.'

Again capital, but not geography for the school."[12]

---

[11] A.W. Andrews and A.J. Herbertson. 1902. "The Geographical Teacher Vol. 1, No. 2." *The Geographical Association.*
[12] A.W. Andrews and A.J. Herbertson. 1902. "The Geographical Teacher Vol. 1, No. 2." *The Geographical Association.*

Redway entered the 20th century solo as well, with a tutorial for teachers entitled *A New Basis for Geography – a Manual for the Preparation of the Teacher* (1901). Lionel Lyde returned with the successful series *Black's School Geography* (1902) in Britain. Herbertson's college text for Oxford made it in as well, and at this time he also released *Man and his Work: An Introduction to Human Geography* (1902), one of the first treatments segregating the human from the physical. The reviewers lauded this work:

"The human element and its central characteristics, whether derived from or worked upon by the environment, are the central theme, and round this are grouped geographical lessons and studies and suggestions galore. Desert and forest, mountain, plain, and coast, agriculture, arts, manufactures, trade and transport, distribution of population, governments, and races- all are properly apportioned according as they are influences modeling nations or effects of geographical causes. To all readers and teachers of geography we commend the book."[13]

Other new works accompanied these. Eliza Morton celebrated the turn of the century by releasing *Potter's New Elementary Geography* (1900). Ralph Tarr and Frank McMurry, who specialized in the physical side, now released *The Complete Geography* (1903). This would be popular in Britain especially, and its major revision a decade later, rebranded *World Geography,* remained so. The American Book Company continued its competitive publications by adding Henry Justin Roddy's *Complete Geography* (1902) to its list of titles, while Rand McNally released Richard Elwood Dodge's *Advanced Geography* (1904). A decade later Dodge would put out an advice book called *The Teaching of Geography in Elementary Schools* (1913).

P.H. L'Estrange's *Progressive Course of Comparative Geography on the Concentric System* (1906) took the whole subject- from simple to advanced- and placed it in one large textbook usable by kids at all levels. If one were going through the subject at one's own pace over an extended period of time, one-room schoolhouse style, this was an ideal textbook to have. In Canada, the government book was still officially sanctioned but not mandatory. Released by the Department of Education twenty years earlier, *The Public School Geography* went through many revisions for half a century. M.F. Maury, who had previously specialized in the geography of the seas and oceans, now released a comprehensive text called *Manual of Geography* (1904). Edward Arnold's *New Shilling Geography with Special Reference to the British Isles and Empire* (1905) was also reviewed by *TGT*:

"This little book is to be recommended if only for its up-to-dateness, notwithstanding the fact that the publishers have seen fit to launch it on the geographical teacher and students dateless. The more's the pity, as it really merits its title; in this year of grace, 1902, at all events it is a 'new' geography. But it has other merits; it is accurate enough for school purposes; it openly demands the concomitant of a good school atlas and supplies one or two sketch maps as supplements thereto; it preserves orthodox modern spelling as laid down by the best geographers; it perpetuates no heresies. We commend, for instance, the introduction of an apt quotation from Mackinder's Britain and the British Seas, *disposing of the old-time 'Gulf Stream myth...' There follows a review of the Earth by continents; in each the British possessions are accorded a chapter to themselves. Here the up-to-dateness is very apparent- witness such proofs as 1901 census figures, geographical results of the Boer War, and notice of the new North-West Frontier Province in India... We heartily commend the book as a good practical geography."*[14]

A new name on the block, McDougall's Educational Company, entered the fray with its *Outlines of Geography* (1908), beginning that company's long tradition hawking social studies material. G. Cecil Fry's *A Textbook of Geography* (1908) would see a couple editions. Foresman, Scott and Co., another

---

[13] A.W. Andrews and A.J. Herbertson. 1902. "The Geographical Teacher Vol. 1, No. 2." *The Geographical Association.*
[14] A.W. Andrews and A.J. Herbertson. 1902. "The Geographical Teacher Vol. 1, No. 2." *The Geographical Association.*

big name, entered the scene with some advice in *The Teaching of Geography* (1909) by William Sutherland, while teachers got more help in *The Teacher's Manual of Object Lessons in Geography* (1902) by Vincent T. Murche, reviewed positively by *TGT*. But it was not a flawless submission:

"The practiced and practical teacher of little ones is self-evident on every page. We cordially therefore recommend it to all who have to take beginner's forms and who are in search of ideas which shall eventually lead to a right understanding of geography... There are a large number of lessons; each is prefixed with a list of articles requisite for illustration; experiments are made; questions and answers elicit information, and the whole is summed up in a few concise sentences. [However], this is a book for teachers couched in children's language, and there is too plentiful a supply of italics *and block type. We protest, too, against the introduction of maps or models which stop short their mapping or modeling at the political frontier of the country under study; nor are we enamored of the constant advice never to draw a map or plain on the upright blackboard, but always to use the author's new 'patented' modeling tray with horizontal blackboard attached. Teachers in search of ideas for budding geographers may safely purchase this book."*[15]

1910s

It was as the new decade began, as the shipyard workers were busy not putting enough lifeboats on the Titanic, that Ellen Churchill Semple used Ratzel's untranslated material as the basis of her own famous work: *Influences of Geographic Environment on the Basis of Ratzel's System of Anthropo-Geography* (1911). Aside from reintroducing Ratzel to the Anglosphere, Semple's analysis was a staple on reading lists in colleges around the empire and in the USA. The year 1911 also saw the release of the *Encyclopedia Britannica 11th edition*, which is still considered the best compendium of Victorian geographic information. It was found in most every university library, and in many preparatory schools. Particularly with this edition, the articles were written by the 'men of action' themselves, i.e.: Freud wrote the article on psychoanalysis and Ford that on mass production. Students would spend hours, nights and weekends reading this encyclopedia. Sometimes they would be brushing up for exams like the Regents, and none too soon. In 1912, the New York Regents came up with new curriculum guidelines for geography classes, meaning back then simply hints on what might be on their test. It was left to individual teachers to get ahold of the revisions and make sure they were up to speed in their classes. That is why The Reliable Company put out *Regents Review in Geography – A Complete Review of the Whole Subject as Outlined in the New Syllabus; Contains all the Regents Questions Adapted to the New Syllabus* (1912). Considering the Regents test inspired the SAT and GRE, and the whole host of exams kids are subjected to today for better or worse, including AP tests, we begin to appreciate these reviews as a kind of ancestor to the review books of today.

Time marched on this decade, and so did the textbooks. First, Charles Dryer's *High School Geography* (1911) appeared. In Britain, B.C. Wallis' *A Geography of the World* (1911) appeared. Salisbury's *Elements of Geography* (1912) appeared. Sir Halford Mackinder, when he found a break from theorizing on geopolitics, teaching courses at Oxford, and climbing Mt. Kenya, wrote a schoolbook- two actually. There was *Our Own Islands: An Elementary Study in Geography* (1913), and *Lands Beyond the Channel: An Elementary Study in Geography* (1913), which together, aimed to present British students with a complete picture. Teachers got some advice from F.L. Holtz' *Principles and Methods of Teaching Geography* (1913), and J. Fairgrieve's *The World Round* (1913), which was published by A&C Black for youngsters. In Britain, aside from the *Britannica,* schools were outfitted with the *Oxford Survey of the British Empire* (1914), edited by Herbertson.

World War I certainly provided a new focus for geographical teaching. Fredrick Mort's *Regional Geography* (1915) was the first new text published during wartime. Maury revised and republished his

---

[15] A.W. Andrews and A.J. Herbertson. 1902. "The Geographical Teacher Vol. 1, No. 2." *The Geographical Association.*

work as *New Complete Geography* (1915), while L'Estrange combined with the Philips Company to produce *Philips' Progressive Atlas of Comparative Geography* (1915) for schools. The American Book Company brought out *Essentials of Geography* (1916) by Brigham and McFarlane, while Henry Holt seemed ahead of his time in publishing *Modern Geography for Schools with Contemporary Tests and Test Schedule* (1917) by Salisbury. The same year, the Detroit Public Schools released *Course of Study in Geography* (1917), an advice book written by a coalition of teachers and principles in the district, who sat in discussion and debate over the course of two years in aid of formulating a sound teaching plan. Unifying the human and physical, it begins poetically with, "Geography is the science of the earth as the home of man."[16] Don't hold your breadth for the revision.

At war's end, geographers were highly influential in resolving issues related to territorial change and how to apportion the lands of the collapsed Austro-Hungarian, Ottoman and German empires, along lines mixing self-determination with the demands of the many emphatic delegations. The American Geographical Society (under the pen of Frederick Teggart) released *Geography as an Aid to Statecraft* (1919) to advise and encourage the diplomats at the Paris Peace Conference. President Isaiah Bowman of the society attended the gathering to oversee the cartographic work done by the American delegation, which was presented as part of the unveiling of President Wilson's Fourteen Points. Later, these maps were used in discussion of the new national borders. As the complex and contentious conference went on, Bowman recorded his thoughts, later to appear in a textbook in which he merged theory with experience, called *The New World: Problems in Political Geography* (1928). Others like Peter Simple took a more lighthearted approach to the subject with *The Giddy Globe- Humorous Geography* (1919).

1920s

Quite a few changes hit with the dawning of the new decade. The Interwar era saw a lot of new titles, a phasing out of many old favorites, and the 'official' branching off of human geography as a separate subject. Jean Brunhes really got the this divergence going with his *Human Geography, an Attempt at a Positive Classification, Principles and Examples* (1920), noted as a foundational text in the field. The path was also cleared by Ellsworth Huntington's celebrated *Principles of Human Geography* (1920), co-authored with Frances Cushing, and Russell J. Smith's series *Human Geography: Peoples and Countries, Regions and Trade* (1921), which was more youth-friendly. Later, Smith reflected on the value of the subject as a whole in *Geography and Our Need of It* (1926). Sorbonne Professor Paul Vidal de la Blache's *Principles of Human Geography* (1926), published by Holt, also became a classic in the field. Vidal de la Blache looked at zooming in on small homogenous regions and describing them in detail. He wanted to find the *genres de vie* (modes of life) of each microregion (which he termed 'pays'), as if one sought to describe the individual pieces of a puzzle, that if fitted together, made up the totality of the human arena of action. He also argued for possibilism, an intellectual modification to Ratzel's more deterministic stance, in which human culture springs from within and is only partly influenced by environment, instead of mostly.

Regular texts came along too. In Britain, the University of London contracted Leonard Brooks to put out *A Regional Geography* (1921) in gradational volumes for schools. These would become quite popular for a decade. Another scholar called Wallace Atwood distributed *New Geography* (1921), and simultaneously released *Teaching the New Geography: A Manuel to Use with the Frye-Atwood Series*, to cover all the bases. Mendel Branom had advice for teachers that favored a hands-on approach in *The Teaching of Geography, emphasizing the project, or active method* (1921). Ernest Young in London took a different tack on youth education in his *Children Far Away: The Homes of Parents and Children in Other Lands* (1921) as part of The Human Geographies series. In Canada, another book was used in schools now, called *A Canadian School Geography* (1922) by George Cornish. This book competed with but did not supplant the government book, however, which sold as well as ever. R.H. Whitbeck's

---

[16] Hathi Trust: http://catalog.hathitrust.org/Record/100076035

High School Geography (1923) was aptly named, while J.F. Unstead made his book, *World Geography and World Problems* (1923), serve to illustrate the 'why' of the present.

Some old favorites made it into the 1920s. The Tarr-McMurry series was still going strong, but now McMurry branched off with his own *Advanced Geography* (1924). Herbertson the man republished his work on man, *Man and His Work*. G. Cecil Fry was republished in 1926, as was Dodge's *Advanced Geography*, and Wallis' book. New ones came up of course, such as E.G. Skeat's *The Principles of Geography Physical and Human* (1926), Mark Jefferson's *Principles of Geography* (1926), published by Harcourt, Brace & Co., Philip Knowlton's *Introduction to World Geography* (1926), published by Macmillan, which became a staple in Britain. To round out the decade, Albert Wilmore's *An Introduction to World Geography* (1929) appeared, and A.W. Andrews' large volume *A Text-Book of Geography* (1929) did as well. Fairgrieve revised his textbook and re-released it as *Geography in School* (1929), which would run through many editions. For kids, *A Child's Geography of the World* (1929) by V.M. Hillyer saw the rounds.

1930s

The 1930s started off where Hillyer left off with book for children like Kay Alice Gertrude's *Adventures in Geography* (1930), and Milton Goldsmith's *Old Mother Earth and Her Family: A Book of Geography for Young People* (1930). The cuteness reached a zenith with Amy Oppenheimer's *A Put-Together Atlas- A Fascinating Pastime that makes Geography Delightful* (1931). The starchy folks at Longmans clearly learned nothing from the trend when they published *The World: A General Geography* (1930) by L. Dudley Stamp, but at least the name was a tad whimsical. Stamp's book went on to become, even so, the standard work of the decade, and in fact Stamp was a great geographer who took on the stupendous task of organizing a land use survey that would've made William the Conqueror proud. He had 250,000 students scour the British landscape and report on how the country's land was being utilized, collected it all into a report, and published it. During WWII, this information would come in handy for the government's direction of the war effort.

With the Great Depression going on, economic geography became more of a focus in textbooks, just as military and war matters were a decade earlier. For a good look at how Britain viewed the world, its dominions and its rivals near the end of the age of empire, *Johnston's New Geography of the World* (1931) by Kermack is a good one to examine. But the big story of the Machine Age was the publication of Hendrik Willem Van Loon's *Geography: The Story of the World We Live In* (1932). Van Loon won the first ever Newbery Medal for his world history book *The Story of Mankind* (1922) a decade earlier, and when he turned his ear from Clio's sweet song to hear the soft whisper of Urania, the academic world's ears perked up too. They were not disappointed. His geography likewise became a favorite in homes and schools, and was revised and reprinted for over 30 years.

In London, John Bygott's *Regional Geography* (1932) made its mark, while another great printer of geography texts, John Wiley, published Earl C. Case's *College Geography* (1932). Another notable publisher, Allyn and Bacon, debuted in the field with *Our World, a Textbook in the New Geography* (1932), by DeForest Stull and Roy Hatch. At Princeton, Richard M. Field's *Principles of Historical Geography from a Regional Point of View* (1933) focused on the past. Still being used in the thirties was Ellsworth Huntington's book, which he revised into a multi-volume series called *Living Geography* (1933), as well as Unstead's book, which was revised into *General and Regional Geography for Students* (1934). Russell Smith's book was popular as ever too, meanwhile, another spinoff was in the making with C. Langdon White's *Geography and Introduction to Human Ecology* (1936).

For perspective's sake, a Soviet textbook by N.N. Baransky called *Geography of the USSR: A Textbook for Middle Schools* (1934), released by the Moscow State Textbook Publishing House at this time- in the middle of the Holodomor in Ukraine and at the outset of the Great Purge throughout the Soviet world-was translated into English. Though not technically a 'worldwide' text, it may be consulted for an interesting perspective on things, and perhaps be contrasted with N. Mikhaylov's *Soviet Geography* (1935), published a year later in Britain by Methuen. Many of the growing plethora of other country-specific geographies, such as Fairgrieve and Young's *Human Geography of the British Empire* (1929), or Carl Sauer's *Man in Nature: America Before the Days of the White Man* (1939), have much merit as well- and Sauer did much to encourage a world regional approach to teaching geography, including defining our modern notion of 'cultural landscape'- but the specificity of regional texts puts them beyond the scope of this retrospective. What isn't beyond our scope is Holland Thompson's supervision of the Grolier Society's *Lands and Peoples* (1930), a seven-volume set reprinted throughout the next forty years. Isaiah Bowman wrote the introduction, and this tour de force was a great addition in the regional line.

Cambridge University Press came onto the scene with its publishing of *The World in Outline: A Text Book of Geography* (1935). Preston E. James' wonderful *Outline of Geography* (1935) appeared too, and became a standard work by the famed geographer of Latin America. In Canada, *A World Geography for Canadian Schools* (1936) by Vernon Denton was published by, interestingly enough if you're into this kind of thing, Dent. Teachers got some more good advice during the decade, this time from D.M. Forsaith, who edited *A Handbook for Geography Teachers* (1932) in Britain, and from E.W. Shanahan, whose *Mapwork and Practical Geography* (1934) contained templates for use in the classroom. James F. Chamberlain took another angle with his *Geography and Society* (1938), which contained much of what human geography texts contain these days. Were it complemented by something like Harvard Professor Derwent Whittlesey's *The Earth and the State: A Study of Political Geography* (1939), or Richard Hartshorne's *Recent Developments in Political Geography* (1935), the bases would be covered.

Hartshorne's other book, *The Nature of Geography; A Critical Survey of Current Thought in the Light of the Past* (1939), was a summary work put forth by the Association of American Geographers, and was the last word on the matter before the opening of World War II. It argued for a lessening of strict environmental determinism and a deeper appreciation of the total 'areal' combination of phenomena in any given place, in aid of seeing the forces working there as an ecological whole. Each place is unique as each region is, and no matter the scale, place will influence people in unique ways. Animate matter then reciprocates and becomes a part of the environment that surrounds it and all the other organisms in the place, which alter the ecology further over time, building environments ever new, altering the environmental inputs of each forthcoming generation.

As the decade broke, a second volume on the value of the subject appeared. Roderick Peattie surprised the public with *Geography in Human Destiny* (1940), about which Ellsworth Huntington said, "This is one of the few books in which a trained geographer of high repute has dared to use all his faculties." What did that mean? While Time Magazine called it "absorbing," and the Boston Globe said, "He took us through the maze of the world and we were entertained and mentally stimulated," while the Scientific Book Club noted, "It stands alone as an integrating philosophy for living, based on a geographic understanding of history," it was Harvard geologist Kirtley F. Mather who saw utility in the book's deepness:

"No one these days can do any intelligent thinking about the numerous problems facing mankind unless he appreciates the intimate relationship between man and his environment. This is one of the best places I know for the layman to get the right attitude of mind and to acquire the needed fund of information regarding that relationship."[17]

---

[17] Peattie, Roderick. 1940. *Geography in Human Destiny*. George W. Stewart.

1940s

Such a perspective was needed in 1940. Like with so many other things, the war years slowed but did not stop the production of geography textbooks. Most books during the later years of the war had smaller margins of empty space to conserve paper, less needless pages, and bore symbols describing the need to be thrifty to help the war effort. Harold Shelton's *Geography and Man* (1940) did not fit this description. It was a sumptuous, 3-volume work bringing together many authors. But if you compare a wartime volume of Van Loon with one before or after, you can see the difference. This didn't affect America until 1942 of course, and in the meantime, Amsco put out an updated Regents review called *Geography Regents Examination Series* (1941). Preston James' *Outline of Geography* (1943) was popular as ever, as was Jasper Stembridge's *The World: A General Regional Geography* (1945). Down under in Australia, Ivor Suymon's *A Modern Geography for Australian Schools* (1943) became the standard work.

Some popular wartime works were Chester Lawrence's *New World Horizons: Geography for the Air Age* (1942), Darrell Davis' *The Earth and Man: A Human Geography* (1943) published by Macmillan, and Vernor Finch's *Elements of Geography: Physical and Cultural* (1942), published by the budding firm McGraw-Hill. A year later George Renner's *Human Geography in the Air Age* (1943) and after that Leonard O. Packard's *Our Air-Age World: A Textbook in Global Geography* (1945), released with humorously similar titles, served to remind us how between the Machine Age and the Nuclear Age, there was a short, oft-forgotten 'Air Age,' when scholars believed future historians would look back on their time and label it after the airplane, the most significant (and cool) feature. 'Atomic Age' quickly took over as a label, which would become 'Space Age' after Sputnik was launched in 1957. When we stopped expanding outward and scrapped the entire space vision by 1975, sociologists variously relabeled the times a 'Postindustrial Age,' a 'Postmodern Age,' an 'Information Age,' a Biotech Era,' etc.

The issue with wartime books describing the world is that everyone knew they'd have to be rewritten as soon as the war was over. Russell Smith gave up and simply called the new edition of his book *Geography and World War II* (1943). When the war did end, a similar situation as after WWI occurred. Previously issued books were replaced, and some old names faded away, but certainly not all. Textbooks as of 1946 simply had a different world to teach about, and new experts emerged. H.A. Calahan's *Geography for Grown-Ups* (1946) published by Harper's, purported to describe, "The wonderment of the world we live on," which might have been a nice comfort around that time. Oxford lent its imprimatur to J.C. Hill's *An Introduction to Geography* (1946).

As for old favorites, Ellsworth Huntington's *Principles of Human Geography*, still the big name in the field, was "largely rewritten" for its 5th edition (1947). The same goes for Renner's book and those of Stembridge, Davis, Shanahan, Stamp, Finch, and the Fairgrieve-Young joint effort. Preston James revised his textbook and rebranded it as *The Geography of Man* (1949). More new books appeared. Rand McNally published W.R. McConnell's *Geography Around the World* (1948), and the Ginn Company in Toronto put out John H. Bradley's *World Geography* (1948). Silver, Burdett and Company published its first textbook, Clarence Sorensen's *A World View: Essential World Geography* (1949), and McGraw-Hill's new work was Otis W. Freeman's *Essentials of Geography* (1949). For 'indy' study, there was *Geography: The World and its People* (1948), published by Odham's.

At the end of the decade, a further trend toward specialization spun off urban geography, which branched off into its own subject area. Imagine each individual chapter in an introductory textbook being its own course- that is what had been accomplished by this time in universities. One could now find books on, in the case of physical and regional geography, Europe, the Soviet sphere, Latin America, Africa, Middle East, Asia, etc., and cartography, while the human geography side had diverged into political, cultural, economic and now urban geography. Walter Christaller pioneered the study of cities in German with his *Central Places in Southern Germany* (1933), as Lewis Mumford did in the English-speaking world with his *The Culture of Cities* (1938). Now in the forties, Methuen published Thomas Griffith Taylor's *Urban Geography* (1949), which did a lot to formalize urban geography as an academic subject. To finish the decade and standardize geographic names and places in English, *Webster's Geographical Dictionary* (1949) became a capstone on the gazetteers of yore.

1950s

As the fifties opened, teachers got some up-to-date advice from Roderick Peattie in *Teaching Geography: A Dynamic Approach* (1950), and later from G.H. Gopsill's *The Teaching of Geography* (1956). The Golden Press, famous for its outreach to children, produced *The Golden Geography: a Child's Introduction to the World* (1950). Munro Leaf also wrote for kids with *Geography Can Be Fun* (1951), while Hillyer's 20-year-old old children's geography was revised and released again. Bigger people got Olive Garnett's *Fundamentals in School Geography* (1951), and really big people got UNESCO's *Geography Teaching for International Understanding* (1951), which they now had to contend with whether they wanted to or not.

For a history of geography's vicissitudes, John Kirtland Wright's *Geography in the Making: The American Geographical Society 1851-1951* (1952) is a worthy insider's look. Noted King's College of London scholars S.W. Wooldridge (geomorphology) and W. Gordon East (historical geography) combined to outline a new vision for the subject in *The Spirit and Purpose of Geography* (1951), a widely read and highly valuable book. For home study, a 3-volume set edited by W.G.V. Balchin called *Geography and Man* (1955) was released. John Bygott revised his 20-year-old textbook into *Introduction to Mapwork and Practical Geography* (1952). The Brunhes, Vidal De La Blache and Stamp texts were also republished, as was McConnell's.

In the fifties, geography as a discipline went into a so-called 'crisis' due to the fact that there was an emphasis on 'vertical' relationships, which were increasingly seen as hierarchical, and a perceived lack of emphasis on horizontal relationships. A *Britannica* article about this crisis referenced critic George Kimble, who said, "Too much effort is spent drawing boundaries that don't exist around areas that don't matter- from the air it is the links in the landscape that impress the observer, not the boundaries."[18] Of course, focus on the horizontal can lead to confusion about geography's scope as a subject. For one, horizontal linkages mean further delineation of subsections and specialties, which could go on ad infinitum, to the point they blend with other subjects enough to cease being a separate entity. For example, should geography be taught as a unified whole or in subsections? If the answer is subsections, like cultural, economic, political, historical etc., then couldn't each section be a component of separate, already existing classes (i.e.: sociology, economics, government, and history)? To answer this, University of Cambridge Professor Jean Brown Mitchell argued historical geography is *geography*, first and foremost, defending the subject in his influential *Historical Geography* (1953).

Another part of the crisis concerned the role of science in geography, because some at the American Geographical Association wanted to refocus the core of the disciple upon quantifiable data patterns, analyzable by scientific method, and the development of geographic laws that would rival those of formulated by geologists, economists, etc. A member named Ackerman even decried the 'Hartshornian' world regional approach as being too descriptive while lacking an aggressive scientific attitude. He favored a positivist approach characterized by data collection and theory-production.[19] Ullman (who formulated laws of trade interaction between two locations) was another leader in this 'new geography' quantitative approach. At the end of this contentious decade (they didn't know what was coming),

---

[18] "Geography as a Science." *Encyclopedia Britannica Online.* Ret. 6/13/15.
[19] Ibid.

Preston James summarized all this in his editing of *New Viewpoints in Geography* (1959), as did Richard Hartshorne in his *Perspective on the Nature of Geography* (1959).

In the meantime, quite a few new textbooks appeared that kept things going as much as possible, such as *Human Geography* (1952) by French geographers M.J. Delamarre and Pierre Deffontaines, both students of Brunhes. There was also *Elements of World Geography* (1953) by Riley Straats, *World Geography: An Introduction* (1954) by Loyal Durand, *World Geography* (1956) edited by George Kish and published by Prentice Hall, and Oliver H. Heintzelman's *World Regional Geography* (1956). The biggest names to release new books were J.H.G. Lebon, whose *An Introduction to Human Geography* (1952) became a major seller, and Arthur Strahler, whose *Physical Geography* (1951) would go through countless editions and become the number one best selling text on specifically physical geography. *World Neighbors: Geography for the Air-Age* (1952) by Juliana Bedier was marketed to Catholic students. E.W.H. Briault's *An Introduction to Advanced Geography* (1957) saw some rounds. Then there was a book entitled *Introduction to Human Geography* (1957), which was written by someone named D.C. Money. The question was whether he was using his dj name or that of his lobbying firm. The Oxford Press put out William S. Roeder's *Visualized World Geography* (1957) but that's not the university press, so be mindful. At the end of the decade, a well known name in publishing today, Barrons, released Guernsey Doerr's *Principles of Geography* (1959), while Allyn and Bacon put out Eugene van Cleef's *Global Geography* (1959).

During the decade, Walt Rostow was thinking about social evolution and developmentalism, and how best to promote positive growth around the world. A more stable world, made so through good trade policy, harnessing the power of capitalism, and limiting corruption, was something that could be shown occurs in a series of phases, as they occur in a society- if the society can manage to make them happen during its social evolution. Basing hiss theory on what he observed in actual societies, "Professor Rostow does not subscribe to the Marxist view that history is uniquely determined by economic forces and motives; instead he offers a comprehensive, realistic and soundly based alternative to Marx' theory of how societies evolve."[20] The result was Rostow's *The Stages of Economic Growth: A Non-Communist Manifesto* (1960), discussed in many geography courses and worthwhile reading, especially if read in combination with Peter Bauer's *Dissent on Development* (1972).

1960s

If the fifties saw a crisis in geography, the sixties saw crisis in everything, and the whole academic system actually did collapse- physically in some places like Paris, Berkeley and Cornell- and almost overnight, the sixties counterculture became the dominant culture in academia. The early sixties, however, saw more of a continuation of the fifties than radical change. In this earlier part, Stamp's book was renewed, D.C. Money was reprinted, James was renewed, Stembridge was renewed, Otis Freeman's quarter-century old work was renewed as *World Geography,* Briault added a new title called *Geography In and Out of School* (1963), and the 6th edition of Bradley's text was republished on its 20th anniversary.

New books on the scene were Frank Debenham's *The McGraw-Hill Illustrated World Geography* (1960), Rhodes Murphey's *Introduction to Geography* (1961), J.S. Hobbs' *General World and Regional Geography: A Revision Course* (1961), and K. Walton's *General Geography* (1965), published by the Grolier Society. Urban geography saw two of its luminary works appear within months of each other: Lewis Mumford's *The City in History* (1961) and Jane Jacob's *The Death and Life of Great American Cities* (1961).

---

[20] Rostow, Walt. 1960. *The Stages of Economic Growth.* Cambridge University Press.

A flurry of human geographies appeared as well. Samuel Newton Dicken's *Introduction to Human Geography* (1963) was a newcomer, while Holt, Reinhart and Winston published George Carter's *Man and the Land: A Cultural Geography* (1963). Chatto & Windus got on the scene by publishing Emrys Jones' *Human Geography* (1963), and Longmans put out both Margaret Reid Shackleton's *Introduction to Human Geography* (1964) and Aime Vincent Perpillou's *Human Geography* (1965). These were all in addition to Lebon's human geo text, which was renewed in 1964 and led the field. McGraw-Hill jumped in too with Jan Otto Marius Broek's *A Geography of Mankind* (1968), and even scholars in far off Rhodesia picked up on the trend, with George Kay releasing *Rhodesia: A Human Geography* (1970).

During this time, teachers got a lot of groovy advice from books like M. Long's *Handbook for Geography Teachers* (1965) published by Methuen, as well as from the National Council for the Social Studies, which put out *Focus on Geography: Key Concepts and Teaching Strategies* (1970), edited by Phillip Bacon. Thomas Walter Freeman, whose *A Hundred Years of Geography* (1962) had became assigned reading at universities, now provided some in-depth advice in *The Geographer's Craft* (1967).

1970s

Seems the seventies had to arrive some time, and they started with a big splash with the release of Harm Jan de Blij's *Geography: Regions and Concepts* (1971), published by Wiley. The most popular textbook since it was published to this very day, it is not an exaggeration to say de Blij cut the path in defining what content is taught and how the curriculum of this subject is delivered today. In that, he occupies a place not unlike Thomas A. Bailey in American History, William H. McNeill in World History, Robert K. Merton in Sociology, and David G. Myers in Psychology. The decade saw more new books than de Blij, in both world and human geography. Works for world geography included a revised Heintzelman text, Jesse Wheeler's *Regional Geography of the World* (1975), and Robert H. Fuson's *Introduction to World Geography: Regions and Cultures* (1977).

In human geography there was a lot of action. Oxford University Press put out *Man, Space and Environment: Concepts in Contemporary Human Geography* (1972), Michael Chisholm's *Studies in Human Geography* (1972) was published by Heinemann, Arthur Guest's *Man and Landscape: A Practical Handbook of Case Studies and Techniques in Human Geography* (1974) appeared, while Broek was back with his text, and Wiley put out Joseph Earle Spencer's *Cultural Geography* (1973). Chisholm, moreover, put the debate over the academic split into the public sphere with his *Human Geography: Evolution or Revolution?* (1975), published by Penguin to an audience of no doubt concerned citizens. St. Martin's Press got into the game with *Human Geography: A Welfare Approach* (1977) by David Marshall Smith, and while Harm de Blij began the decade with his classic world regional geography, now came his other big splash, *Human Geography: Culture, Society and Space* (1977). Again published by Wiley, this book did its part to systematize the curriculum, and became the bestselling human geography text into the new millennium. Finally, HarperCollins really wanted into the game, releasing two titles within a year of each other. First it was W.V. Tidswell's *Pattern and Process in Human Geography* (1978), then Charles Whynne-Hammond's *Elements of Human Geography* (1979).

Practical help for teachers- what would they think of next- came from Macmillan, which published *Outline Maps for World Human Geography* (1972). Molly Long's *Handbook for Geography Teachers* (1974) along with David Hall's *Geography and the Geography Teacher* (1976), meanwhile, were both published by Allen & Unwin. These, along with Philip Boden's *Developments in Geography Teaching* (1976), all reached the shelves. And that wasn't all. At the end of the decade came *Place and People: A Guide to Modern Geography Teaching* (1979) by Stewart Dunlop.

Ask an unsuspecting consenting adult the following two questions: "How many textbooks does the average American read after they finish with school?" and "How many textbooks have you read since you finished school?" They may guess something like "a few" for the first one, and the answer to the second one is probably going to be zero, or, "uh, none." There is a terrible statistic that has been floating around that the answer really is zero. Urban legend? Maybe, but it is possible- you'd have to survey many thousands of out-of-schoolers and ascertain whether under half of one percent read textbooks, which would round down to zero. Controlling for teachers and profs, your hypothetical interviewee might say, "well, textbooks are boring, what do you expect?" And it may be true. School kids consume them because they are, in effect, a captive audience- not exactly free market forces at work. Thus, books for the general public usually have a little more pizzazz, and this may hold for some geography books as well. Case-in-point is a wonderful, even sublime book about the meaning of the subject, which was read throughout the seventies and beyond. Preston E. James' exposition of the grand ideas of the past, and their relation to the society of the present, was called *All Possible Worlds: A History of Geographic Ideas* (1972). A magnum opus after a lifetime of learning, it is one of the few books without a brand new glossy cover that is still recommended reading on many university course lists. You *could* read something more specific, like a UNESCO report on hydrology from the Baniff Symposia of 1972, which going at the same time *All Possible Worlds* was released, but if you are on a time budget like most earth life, discrimination is recommended.

1980s

In the 1980s, D.C. Money's two-decade-old *Basic Geography* was reminted, and Longmans released Arild Holt-Jensen's *Geography: It's History and Concepts* (1980). Gerald A. Danzer's *Land and People: A World Geography* (1982) was an addition by Scott, Foresman & Co, but the big story was the release of Paul Ward English's *World Regional Geography* (1984). It became de Blij's number one competitor for the decade, and put out by the same firm- good call Wiley. Meanwhile, the venerable Preston E. James spent his last year on earth producing his last textbook about it: *World Geography* (1985). At least he didn't mince words, and neither did Richard Bergeron, whose *World Geography* (1986) was published by Allyn and Bacon. William Marsh's *Earthscape* (1986) gets points for coolest title. Finally, we have Gary Manson's *World Geography* (1989), released by McGraw-Hill, David G. Armstrong's *World Geography: People and Places* (1989), released by Merrill, and David L. Helgren's *World Geography Today* (1989), released by Holt.

Teachers were treated to a Western Michigan University study called *Teacher Education Models in Geography: An International Comparison* (1984), which purported to demonstrate the different strategies used in various countries. At this point, most textbooks came with teacher's editions that contained specialized hints and guides anyway. For a different way to see human geography, however, teachers of the eighties could locate *The Stamp Atlas: A unique assembly of geography, social & political history, and postal information* (1986) by John Flower. Since they couldn't just, say, go online and look at stamps from different nations demonstrating geography themes (hint, hint), having a book with them was quite handy.

In urban geography, two books of note appeared. One, Hohenberg and Lees' *The Making of Urban Europe* (1985), published by Harvard University Press, was a major study in how cities have grown and changed. A little friendlier is Mark Girouard's *Cities & People* (1985), published by Yale, which takes a snapshot approach. It selects key cities to illustrate each phase of urban growth since 1000. And it has pictures.

Human geographies certainly did well in the eighties, as they did in the seventies. In Britain, Patrick McBride's *Human Geography* (1980) got the Blackie publishing house into the game, while McGraw-Hill released a new edition of Broek's *Geography of Mankind,* and Weidenfeld and Nicolson, a venerable publisher, entered the field with *Introduction to Human Geography* (1982) by Ian Hopkins. But the big story of the mid-80s was the release of James M. Rubenstein's *The Cultural Landscape* (1983) by a smaller firm, Brooks/Cole. This is significant because while Rubenstein's textbook would start out slow, it would eventually make it to the very top of the pack on internal merit, running neck and neck with de Blij throughout the 2000s. And the decade was not nearly over. Next, Longmans put out *People on Earth: Human Geography* (1984) by Ian Jackson and Roger Robinson, Harper and Row put out *Human Mosaic: A Thematic Approach to Cultural Geography* (1986), and Prentice Hall countered these with Robert Stoddard's *Human Georgraphy: People, Places and Cultures* (1986). In Britain, Palgrave-Macmillan anted up by releasing *Horizons in Human Geography* (1989) by Walford and Gregory, and Routledge met them by putting out both A. Kobayashi's *Remaking Human Geography* (1989) and Peter Jackson's *Maps of Meaning: An Introduction to Cultural Geography* (1989).

1990s

All would be out of date overnight, because on Christmas Day 1991, the Soviet government voted itself out existence and the Cold War was over. The bi-polar world, as it had been described by geographers since the 1940s, was now unipolar and soon to be multipolar, and as of January 1992, text had to be rewritten and maps revised. At the same time maybe it didn't matter that much, because one of the biggest sellers in geography that year was *Don't Know Much About Geography: Everything You Need To Know About The World But Never Learned* (1991) by Kenneth C. Davis. We'll blame that one on the libraries. But it reflected a growing recognition, especially in America, that the geographic understanding of the average citizen was a bit lacking, despite the mass purchasing by school districts of books like Holt's *World Geography Today* (1991), now authored primarily by Robert Sager, Edward Bergman's *Introduction to Geography* (1991), published by Prentice Hall, Richard Boehm's *Glencoe World Geography* (1992), Wynn Kapit's *Geography Coloring Book* (1991), and well, you get the picture. But the answer was nigh: harness the magic of the Five Themes! And lo, choice morsels like *Unlocking the Five Themes of Geography* (1999) and *Teaching the Five Themes* (2001) talked up what the themes were all about, and how to fill students minds with their permutations, chapter-by-chapter. But they didn't talk very much about why you *should*. This represented a greater trend throughout the social sciences to replace content knowledge with a specific pattern of thinking- meaning learning how to think a certain way- mostly leading to a lack of thinking period.

Teachers got some help from a few places outside T.E.'s as well (we have to use the acronym so students don't know what we are talking about). From the Center for Applied Research in Education, whose materials could be found at supply outlets, teachers got some practical assignments in *Ready-To-Use World Geography Activities for Grades 5-12* (1992). From Prentice Hall they received *Geography for Educators: Standards, Themes and Concepts* (1995), which surely helped inspire something, but what it might have been may forever remain a mystery. From Scholastic they got *Geography: A Practical Guide to Teaching Within the National Curriculum* (1996). This period was also the fever pitch of the bloc-scheduling craze, and it was Glencoe to the rescue with *Geography: The World and Its People: Block Scheduling Implementation Guide* (1997). Like usual, kids got better things than the big people did. Dorling Kindersley (DK), well known for their sumptuous volumes full of great pictures and text presented in a modular fashion, brought out *Geography of the World* (1996), while Margaret Kenda's *Geography Wizardry for Kids* (1997) was a nice touch from Barrons.

The dominant books of the nineties were de Blij's *Realms, Regions and Concepts* (the 8th edition of which celebrated its silver anniversary by adding 'Realms' to the title) and the Rubenstein text. Paul Ward English's book did well too. It was re-released on its 10th anniversary as *Geography: People and Places* (1994). Prentice Hall went for more market share by hitting the nos and releasing David Clawson's *World Regional Geography* (1997), and *World Geography: Building a Global Perspective* (1998), by Thomas J. Baerwald and Celeste Fraser. Christopher Salter's *Essentials of World Regional Geography* (1999) was also in play. In Britain, R. James Crewe's *World Geography* (1998) released by Oxford University Press was well used, along with Paul Guinness' *Advanced Geography: Concepts and Cases* (1999). Another college text was Michael Bradshaw's *The New Global Order: A World Regional Geography* (1999).

On the human geography side, there was William Norton's *Human Geography* (1992), and Kent and Bradford's *Understanding Human Geography* (1992), both authoritative texts published by Oxford University Press. An interesting title on the cultural geography branch was *Exploring Music through Geography* (1993) by Wheway and Thomson. Later in the decade, Paul L. Knox and Sallie Marston's *Places and Regions in Global Context: A Human Geography* (1997) made its appearance. Roger Berry's *Into all the World: A Christian Text on World Geography* (1991), Pamela Creason's *Geography for Christian Schools* (1994), and Michael D. Matthews' *Geography: For Christian Schools* (1998) attracted private school accounts but not many yeshivas or madrassas. The CSI team is looking into it.

In urban geography, two highly readable works appeared, of the kind that entertain while educating. Joel Garreau provided some insight into the suburban 'downtowns' and the otherworldly phenomenon of office parks rising from the cornfields in *Edge City* (1991), while James Howard Knustler's *The Geography of Nowhere: The Rise and Decline of America's Manmade Landscape* (1993) was a bit of a downer but basically said 'we've hit bottom via building an alienated landscape, and the only way out is up.' Let's hope he's right.

2000s

The year 2000, known as Y2K at the time, was one of anticipation. The new millennium was here, a new millennium of giant publishers dominating the market while- perhaps ironically- the Internet democratized the communication of knowledge. As far as textbooks go, districts and teachers actually had less to choose from, due to high stakes testing, an overall move to centralization, and a rather complacent trend to uniformity seen throughout the curriculum, governed by 'standards upon standards' from every level of government plus special interest groups and political action committees. 'The sage on the stage,' as they said, had to morph into 'the guide on the side.' But that was only half of the story. If the teacher was no longer to be a source of content and interpretation so much as a 'friend helping out friends learn stuff,' it didn't mean there was no longer a source for the content. The source simply went up a few levels to the textbook writers, curriculum designers and standards masters, who collectively said, aping their favorite President, "We're the Decider."

The result? The decade's biggest seller for high schools, *Glencoe World Geography* (2000), was a brightly colored but thoroughly vacuous production, equivalent to the many world history textbooks written on World Systems Theory. Unnervingly similar and only marginally better were Holt, Reinhart and Winston's *World Geography Today* (2000), and McDougal Littell's *World Geography* (2002). Some teachers and professors turned to assigning more inspiring non-textbooks, for example DK volumes covering parts of the geographic spectrum, like *Earth* (2003), which contained physical and urban geography, and *Human* (2004), which contained human geography (and some anatomy, government, psychology and sociology to boot).

At the university level, De Blij's *Regions* was still king of the campus. McBride's *Human Geography* was republished (2004) by Blackie for the British market, while the very long running text *Physical Geography*- first published back in 1951 by Arthur Strahler- was revised by Alan Strahler and released by Wiley under the slightly modified title: *Introducing Physical Geography* (2004). If anyone is keeping longevity records, this one has got to be up there.

As for human geography, Peter Daniels' *Human Geography* (2002) published by Prentice Hall was a nice edition, while Jerome Fellmann edited a few editions of McGraw-Hill's *Landscapes of Human Activities* (2005), featuring Jon C. Malinowski and Arthur and Judith Getis. Rubenstein's *The Cultural Landscape,* which appeared in new editions in 2005 and 2008, shared the top spot with de Blij, who now had Alexander B. Murphy and Erin Fouberg as co-authors. The Knox-Marston text was still available (2006), as were the Baerwald (2007), Norton (2007) and Bradshaw (2008) texts.

If that sounds like a lot, the big news of the decade was that in 2001, the College Board inaugurated the first course in Advanced Placement Human Geography, opening a wider market for textbooks. Alec Murphy- the de Blij co-writer- was a leading force in the drive to make the class happen, and he was supported by many other names mentioned herein. The windfall behind the ultimate success of getting this class is hard to overestimate. The geographical literacy of the public is well served by it for many reasons- it actually is a really good advanced course that gets kids excited about geography, conveying necessary and vital content for comprehension of and success in the modern world.

The addition of AP Human Geography to the College Board curriculum helped spur another change- review books became a growth stock, a bubble that actually didn't burst by the end of the decade. Princeton Review's *Cracking the Regents: Global History and Geography* (2000) helped kick-start the review book craze. In 2003, Barrons expanded into the AP Human Geography market, with its *How to Prepare for the AP Human Geography Advanced Placement Examination* (2003). Princeton Review followed suit a year later, and Kaplan released one in 2007 by noted curriculum designer Kelly Swanson. A review aiming for the general public was *An Idiot's Guide to Geography* (2004) by Joseph Gonzalez. Teachers, meanwhile, got help from Margaret Smith in *Aspects of Teaching Secondary Geography: Perspectives on Practice* (2002), published by Routledge, and online at the College Board website. About the subject as a whole, Norman Graves did interested teachers a service by writing *School Text Book Research: The Case of Geography 1800-2000* (2001). According to the preface, its goal was to highlight the history of the subject as it had been taught in British schools:

"This book is an analysis of the evolution of geography textbooks in use in the United Kingdom from 1800 to the end of the 20th century. The author assesses the influence of geographical and scientific ideas, of pedagogical theories and practices of the cultural ethos of society and of technological change on the production and publication of textbooks. The battle of ideas is ever present: physical scientists compete with Mackinderite geographers for supremacy at the turn of the 19th century; conceptual revolutionaries and quantitative geographers battle with regional and humanistic specialists in the 1960s and 1970s. These intellectual skirmishes are represented in the textbooks produced. But so are the wider issues within society: imperialism, racial bias, sexism and prejudices of various kinds. The author argues that textbooks reflect society, but they tend to follow changes rather than lead them."[21]

Another one to look for on the history of textbooks in schools- how they have been selected and why- is William E. Marsden's *The School Textbook* (2001), published by Routledge.

At the end of the decade, de Blij brought out a recommendable book of his own, semi-autobiographical, that went into some issues in more detail. Called *The Power of Place* (2009), Bill Moyers said of it: "What Carl Sagan did for cosmology, Harm de Blij is doing for geography. See, hear, or read him and you will sign on for a continuing course in a subject that he had brought alive like no one else in our time. *The Power of Place* is one of those books I hope the next President will read."[22]

2010s

Our own decade has seen the markets for on-level geography, AP Human Geography, and college geography become more competitive than ever- big money, this. Luckily, geography textbooks are, on a whole, quite superior to those in other social sciences, but you have to be selective. In teacher resources and review guides for students, the Princeton Review, Kaplan, Barrons, 5-Steps-to-a-5 by Carol Ann Gillespie, and others run a steady racket. Regarding new textbooks, one from a merged Holt-McDougal appeared, called *Geography* (2012), the name perhaps indicating a 'back to basics' approach. Joseph

---

[21] Graves, Norman. 2001. *School Textbook Research: The Case of Geography.* Institute of Education.
[22] De Blij, Harm J. 2009. *The Power of Place.* John Wiley and Sons.

Hobbs' *Fundamentals of World Regional Geography* (2012) published by Prentice Hall, is an up and coming title. Dahlman's *Introduction to Geography* (2013) and Alyson Greiner's *Visualizing Geography: At Home in a Diverse World* (2014) are new on the scene as well.

They have an uphill battle. Old favorites are doing well as ever. De Blij's *Geography: Realms, Regions and Concepts* (2013), co-authored by Peter O. Muller and Jan Nijman, and now adorned simply with the title *REGIONS* in big font, still leads in world geography by a wide margin. Its 16th edition, however, will be the last authored by de Blij, who passed on to meet the Great Geographer in the sky not long after it the presses. *Understanding World Regional Geography* (2015) is a new one from Fouberg and William G. Moseley. The Knox-Marston text remains available, and Bradshaw's *World Regional Geography* (2014) is still in play, now co-written by White, Dymond, Chacko, and Scheidt. Getis' *Introduction to Geography* (2013) is in its 14th edition and doing fine, and Guinness' book is too, rebranded *IB Diploma Geography* (2012). Garrett Nagle's *IB Geography Coursebook* (2012) is another to look at for that program. On the physical side, Strahler motors on, and de Blij and Muller's *Physical Geography* does as well, twin titans in a physical-material world. *Glencoe World Geography* (2013) is back too, targeting more modest achievers. In urban studies, Edward Glaeser's *Triumph of the City* (2011) challenges Jane Jacobs' ideal (it seems no one has in fifty years).

In human geography, the Getis, Getis, Fellmann, Bjelland, Montello team effort *Human Geography: Landscapes of Human Activities* (2012) remains available in its 12th edition, while Robert F. Ritchie's *Human Geography: An Interactive Approach from a Christian World-View* (2012) is a new one to check out for that market. They to have an uphill battle too, because at the top of the heap are books of enduring value. Rubenstein's *The Cultural Landscape 11th edition* (2013), published by Prentice Hall (for which this *Tamm's Textbook Tools* was done), is both well written and has compelling illustrations. However, it has become markedly more politicized since the 10th edition, which was quite better, and many important names have been removed (Friedrich Ratzel, Halford Mackinder, Nicholas Spykman, etc.). If you can get by those things, it is a good textbook. Right there at the top with Rubenstein is the venerable *Human Geography: People, Place and Culture* (2015), by de Blij, Fouberg and Murphy. Now also in its 11th edition, this book, dating from 1977, is six years older than *The Cultural Landscape* but currently in the same edition. Go figure. Both of these, along with the very promising 1st edition of Jon C. Malinowski and David H. Kaplan's *Human Geography* (2013), which bests the rest on geography's history and is presented in modules, are better than most textbooks you will find across the social sciences. Relatively- but not totally- free of spin, all of them at least focus on the subject at hand.

Here ends this treatment of books used to teach students geography. For a last recommendation, seek out the surprise of the decade: Aleksandra Mizielinska and Daniel Mizielinski's *Maps* (2013) with activity book. No matter your age or that of your students, you won't regret it. In the end, after all, it's the books that matter. They are what matter when the power goes out; they are what matter when the power is on. They carry on the conversation of the centuries.

David Tamm
Summer Vacation
2015

INDEX OF AUTHORS

Year	Author	Year	Author	Year	Author
1570	Abraham Ortelius	1860	Alex Keith Johnston	1904	M.F. Maury
1625	Nathanial Carpenter	1861	George Hodgins	1905	Edward Arnold
1650	Bernhardus Varenius	1861	S.S. Cornell	1906	P.H. L'Estrange
1652	Peter Heylyn	1862	James Monteith	1908	T. Athol Joyce
1693	Johan Hubner	1863	Robert Anderson	1908	N.W. Thomas
1701	Herman Moll	1864	George Perkins Marsh	1908	McDougall's
1716	Patrick Gordon	1866	Arnold Henry Guyot	1908	G. Cecil Fry
1726	Isaac Watts	1867	Thomas Sledgwick Fay	1911	Ellen Churchill Semple
1754	Anton Friedrich Busching	1868	D.M. Warren	1911	Charles Dryer
1760	William Guthrie	1869	J.M.D. Meiklejohn	1911	B.C. Wallis
1777	Charles Middleton	1870	Adolf von Steinwehr	1912	Rollin D. Salisbury
1780	Richard Turner	1872	J.B. Calkins	1913	Halford Mackinder
1783	Richard Gadesby	1873	Viscount Bryce	1913	J. Fairgrieve
1783	George Millar	1875	George Gill	1915	Fredrick Mort
1789	Jedidiah Morse	1876	Harper's	1916	Albert Brigham
1796	Nathanial Dwight	1876	William Swinton	1916	Charles McFarlane
1797	Nicholas Dufresnoy	1878	Elisee Reclus	1919	Peter Simple
1798	John Pinkerton	1878	E.G. Ravenstein	1920	Jean Brunhes
1803	J. Goldsmith	1878	Augustus Henry Keane	1920	Ellsworth Huntington
1805	Susanna Rowson	1879	William Hughes	1920	Frances Cushing
1807	Elijah Parish	1880	J. Richardson	1921	Russell J. Smith
1807	Richard Phillips	1881	George F. Cram	1921	Leonard Brooks
1809	E.G. Spafford	1881	Carl Ritter	1921	Wallace Atwood
1810	Benjamin Davies	1882	Edwin Houston	1921	Ernest Young
1810	Joseph Guy	1883	D.G. Brinton	1922	George Cornish
1813	Jacob Cummings	1885	Cassell's	1923	R.H. Whitbeck
1813	Samuel Butler	1887	Jacques Redway	1923	U.F. Unstead
1813	Rodolphus Dickenson	1887	D.A. Chase	1926	Paul Vidal de la Blache
1816	Christopher Kelly	1887	Dept. of Education	1926	E.G. Skeat
1816	E. Mackenzie	1888	A. Buckley	1926	Mark Jefferson
1816	Daniel Adams	1888	Edward Strickland	1926	Philip Knowlton
1819	Joseph Worcester	1888	Friedrich Ratzel	1928	Isaiah Bowman
1823	Sidney Morse	1889	J.D. Quackenbos	1929	Albert Wilmore
1825	Walter Bromley	1889	Charles F. King	1929	V.M. Hillyer
1826	Conrad Malte-Brun	1893	George Chisholm	1930	Holland Thompson
1827	Samuel G. Goodrich	1893	John Clark Ridpath	1930	Kay Alice Gertrude
1827	Peter Parley	1894	James A. Bowen	1930	Milton Goldsmith
1828	James Bell	1895	Alex Everett Frye	1930	L. Dudley Stamp
1828	Ingram Cobbins	1895	H.O. Arnold-Forster	1931	W.R. Kermack
1828	Thomas Ewing	1896	Robert Sullivan	1932	Hendrik Van Loon
1830	Nathan Hale	1896	Lionel Lyde	1932	John Bygott
1831	James Olney	1896	Horace Tarbell	1932	Earl C. Case
1833	James J. Clute	1896	William Sadlier	1932	DeForest Stull
1834	J.L. Blake	1898	Andrew Herbertson	1932	Roy Hatch
1835	Roswell Smith	1898	Russell Hinman	1933	Walter Christaller
1835	Alexander Stewart	1898	Charles Bird	1933	Richard M. Field
1836	Thomas Smiley	1898	James Clyde	1934	N.N. Baransky
1838	Nathanial Huntington	1899	John Keane	1935	N. Mikhaylov
1839	Aaron Arrowsmith	1899	William Morris Davis	1935	Cambridge
1840	Samuel Augustus Mitchell	1899	H.R. Mill	1935	Preston E. James
1845	Alexander von Humboldt	1900	Eliza Morton	1936	C. Langdon White
1846	John Bartholomew	1902	J.B. Reynolds	1936	Vernon Denton
1847	Sylvester Bliss	1902	Henry Justin Roddy	1938	Lewis Mumford
1855	Francis McNally	1903	Ralph S. Tarr	1939	Carl Sauer
1856	Samuel Maunder	1903	Frank McMurry	1939	Richard Hartshorne
1856	E.E. White	1904	Richard Elwood Dodge	1939	Derwent Whittlesey

Year	Name	Year	Name	Year	Name
1940	Roderick Peattie	1975	Jesse Wheeler	2013	Jon C. Malinowski
1940	Harold Shelton	1977	Robert H. Fuson	2013	David H. Kaplan
1942	Chester Lawrence	1977	David Marshall Smith	2013	Aleksandra Mizielinska
1942	Vernor Finch	1978	W.V. Tidswell	2020	You?
1943	Darrell Davis	1979	Charles Whynne-Hammond		
1943	Ivor Suymon	1980	Arlid Holt-Jensen		
1943	George Renner	1980	Patrick McBride		
1945	Jasper Stembridge	1982	Gerald A. Danzer		
1946	H.A. Callahan	1982	Ian Hopkins		
1946	J.C. Hill	1983	James M. Rubenstein		
1948	W.R. McConnell	1984	Paul Ward English		
1948	John H. Bradley	1984	Ian Jackson		
1948	Odham's	1984	Roger Robinson		
1949	Clarence Sorensen	1986	Robert Stoddard		
1949	Otis Freeman	1986	William Marsh		
1949	Thomas Griffith Taylor	1986	Richard Bergeron		
1950	Golden Press's	1989	Gary Manson		
1951	Munro Leaf	1989	David G. Armstrong		
1951	S.W. Wooldridge	1989	David L. Helgren		
1951	W. Gordon East	1989	Red Walford		
1951	Arthur Strahler	1989	Derek Gregory		
1952	Juliana Bedier	1989	A. Kobayashi		
1952	John Kirtland Wright	1989	Peter Jackson		
1952	M.J. Delamarre	1991	Kenneth C. Davis		
1952	Pierre Deffontaines	1991	Robert Sager		
1952	J.H.G Lebon	1991	Roger Berry		
1953	Jean Brown Mitchell	1991	Edward Bergman		
1953	Riley Straats	1991	Joel Garreau		
1954	Loyal Durand	1992	Richard Boehm		
1955	W.G.V. Balchin	1992	William Norton		
1956	George Kish	1993	James Howard Knustler		
1956	Oliver H. Heintzelman	1994	Pamela Creason		
1957	E.W.H. Briault	1997	David Clawson		
1957	D.C. Money	1997	Paul L. Knox		
1957	William S. Roeder	1997	Sallie Marston		
1959	Guernsey Doerr	1998	Michael D. Matthews		
1959	Eugene van Cleef	1998	Thomas J. Baerwald		
1960	Walt Rostow	1998	Celeste Fraser		
1960	Frank Debenham	1998	R. James Crewe		
1961	Rhodes Murphey	1998	Peter O. Muller		
1961	J.S. Hobbs	1999	Paul Guinness		
1961	Jane Jacobs	1999	Michael Bradshaw		
1962	Thomas Walter Freeman	2002	Paul Daniels		
1963	Samuel Newton Dicken	2003	Dorling Kindersley		
1963	George Carter	2004	Joseph Gonzalez		
1963	Emrys Jones	2005	Jerome Fellmann		
1964	Margaret Reid Shakleton	2005	Arthur Getis		
1965	Aime Perpillou	2005	Judith Getis		
1965	K. Walton	2007	Alec Murphy		
1968	Jan Otto Marius Broek	2007	Kelly Swanson		
1970	George Kay	2010	William G. Moseley		
1971	Harm Jan de Blij	2010	Erin Fouberg		
1972	Oxford's	2012	Joseph Hobbs		
1972	Michael Chisholm	2012	Garrett Nagle		
1973	Joseph Earle	2012	Robert F. Ritchie		
1974	Arthur Guest	2013	Jan Nijman		

Thank You!

If this resource book has no use for you, it has no value. We strive to make materials you can actually *use,* with no waste, no filler (unless you didn't like the geography essay), only usable resources with minimal marginalia aligned with the course for convenience. This is how the *Tamm's Textbook Tools* system works:

Coursepak A, this one, has daily assignments for Monday and Tuesday (or two other days of the week, however you work it). It has the vocab, people and chapter assignment packets.

Coursepak B, coming up on *Amazon* and elsewhere else will have material that can be used two other days during the week. This time the focus is reading comprehension, online activities, short answers and Free Response Questions (FRQs). Sometimes these take the form of document analysis (DBQs) and other best practices-type stuff.

Coursepak C, *The Grand Tour* series, is the part of the *Tamm's Textbook Tools* line that stretches across the disciplines. If you were interested in geography, you would look for *The Grand Tour of Geography*. If you were doing a world history class, you'd look for *The Grand Tour of World History.* All *Grand Tours* weave in material from a variety of subjects in the way your subject relates to them. By presenting the big moments in the history and development of your subject in a cross-curricular way, math and science are discussed in social studies courses, pleasing administrators and team-teaching folks. As the big moments are presented, students are asked to respond to them. They are asked to do this objectively at times, subjectively at others. Care has been taken to ensure the *Grand Tour* series of workbooks are done in a way that makes students feel like they are part of the great conversation, with the overall aim of kindling or rekindling excitement for the topic, all aligned with the curriculum. It's worth a try!

Look for these and more in the *Tamm's Textbook Tools* series, a low-cost, timesaving way to find high quality, custom materials tailor made to textbooks in many different subjects. Contact the marketing department anytime with suggestions, corrections and any other correspondence at hudsonfla@gmail.com. Find *TTT* on Facebook as well.

© 2016 David Tamm

Made in the USA
Lexington, KY
19 October 2017